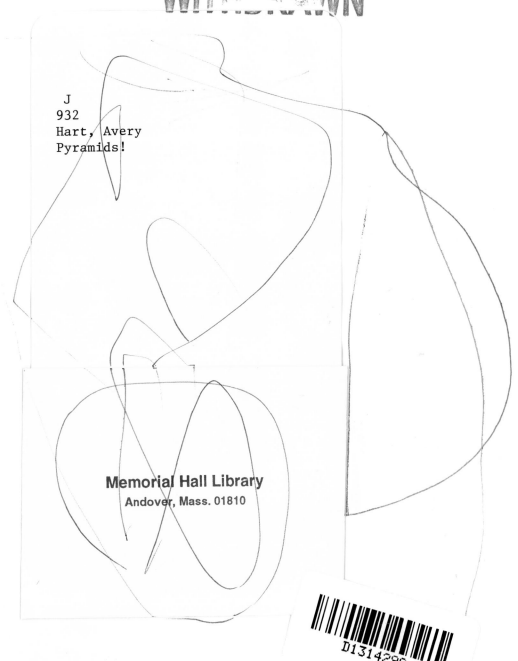

"... a gold mine of ideas for teachers and a playground of Egyptian culture for kids."
— American Library Association *Booklist*

PYRAMIDS!

Winner
of the

*Children's Book Council
Notable Book Award*

and

*Dr. Toy 10 Best
Educational Products*

A WILLIAMSON *KALEIDOSCOPE KIDS*® BOOK

This book is for children who like to wonder, especially the wonderful children of Ringwood and Montclair, NJ.

Williamson Publishing Books by Avery Hart and Paul Mantell:

ANCIENT ROME!
Exploring the Culture, People & Ideas of This Powerful Empire
with Sandra Gallagher

ANCIENT GREECE!
40 Hands-On Activities to Experience This Wondrous Age

KNIGHTS & CASTLES
50 Hands-On Activities to Experience the Middle Ages

BOREDOM BUSTERS!
The Curious Kids' Activity Book

KIDS MAKE MUSIC!
Clapping & Tapping from Bach to Rock

KIDS GARDEN!
The Anytime, Anyplace Guide to Sowing & Growing Fun

Copyright © 1997 by Avery Hart and Paul Mantell

All rights reserved.

No portion of this book may be reproduced mechanically, electronically, or by any other means including photocopying or on the Internet without written permission of the publisher.

Kids Can!®, Little Hands®, Kaleidoscope Kids®, Quick Starts for Kids!®, and Tales Alive® are registered trademarks of Williamson Publishing Company.

Good Times™ is a trademark of Williamson Publishing Company.

Library of Congress Cataloging-in-Publication Data

Hart, Avery.
   Pyramids!: 50 hands-on activities to experience ancient Egypt/ by Avery Hart & Paul Mantell.
   p. cm.
   Includes index.
   ISBN 1-885593-10-4
   1. Egypt–Civilization–to 332B.C.–Juvenile literature.
   I. Mantell, Paul. II. Title.
   DT61. H283 1997
   932–dc21   96-40033
                              CIP

Cover design: **Joseph Lee Design, Inc.**
Interior design: **Joseph Lee Design, Inc.**
Illustrations: **Michael Kline Illustration**
Printing: **Quebecor Printing, Inc.**

Photographs: **Laurie Platt Winfrey, Inc.**
Pages: cover (4), 44, 62, 64, 84, 89.

Printed in Canada

Williamson Publishing Co.
P.O. Box 185
Charlotte, Vermont 05445
1-800-234-8791

10 9 8 7 6

PYRAMIDS!

50 HANDS-ON ACTIVITIES TO EXPERIENCE ANCIENT EGYPT

Avery Hart & Paul Mantell

Illustrations by
Michael Kline

WILLIAMSON PUBLISHING • CHARLOTTE, VT

CONTENTS

J
932
Har

Ancient Egypt: Where Magic and Mystery Meet

The pyramids of ancient Egypt are awesome reminders of the fascinating people who lived on the banks of the flowing Nile River thousands of years ago.

Created before the days of steel or plastic, before electricity, engines, bulldozers, trucks, computers, telephones, and even money, these man-made mountains of stone cause us to wonder:

- Why were the pyramids built?
- How could these enormous structures have been built without modern-day machinery and technology?
- What sort of people created them? Did they use slaves to build them?
- Who paid for them?
- And are the rumors of the pyramids' secret, magical powers really true?

To find out, we'll explore the past and make it come alive again. We'll experience life as a child of ancient Egypt and we'll ask questions about what we experience. We'll use arts, crafts, thinking, costumes, games, math, poems, and stories to catapult ourselves back in time. And there, in the ancient past, we'll find some answers hidden in treasures unlike any of today—treasures of mystery, beauty, and magic.

A Kid Is Still a Kid

WHO WERE THE PEOPLE OF ANCIENT EGYPT?

It's amazing to think that the sun, moon, and stars that shine down on us are the very same as those that shone on the people of ancient Egypt thousands of years ago. Egyptian kids felt breezes and the warmth of the sun just as we do today. They saw birds flying through the air and beetles crawling on the earth, too. But these ancients, as the people of old Egypt are called, had very different ideas about nature, the world around them, and about how the universe worked.

Sometimes we modern people think that people who lived long ago didn't know much. But the truth is, some ancient societies were very advanced in many ways. Would you believe that Egyptian doctors of ancient times successfully performed brain surgery? Or, that Egyptians could predict the exact time of a flood? And it's plain to see that the pyramids, with their exacting construction and awesome design, are every bit as beautiful as the steel and glass buildings of today. So, one of the bonds between the yesterdays of long ago and today is that people across time have been creative thinkers and exacting artisans.

ERASE THESE

Imagine being alive in ancient times, perhaps 5,000 years ago. What would your life be like? How would it be the same as your life today, and how would it be different? You can begin finding out by marking an X in some magazines on anything you see pictured that did not exist long ago.

You'll need a stack of old magazines (try different kinds—news, sports, garden) and a black marker. As you cross things out, imagine living without them. Will you miss cars, bikes,

Think About It:

Money! Some people want more and other people think it causes most of the problems in our world today. Do you think the Egyptians had the right idea in creating a society without money?

telephones, computers, supermarkets, airplanes, TVs, tape recorders, and air-conditioning? While you're at it, make the earth happy and forget about food coloring, plastic, pesticides, and even money! And, what will seem really strange to us—the people of old Egypt didn't miss any of those things!

But don't cross out rope, string, bowling, jewelry, headbands, balls, parties, pastries, music, dancing, or writing. These creations of ancient Egypt are still very much a part of our lives today.

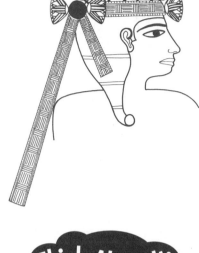

THEN & NOW

Think About It:

*T*oday, most of us know that kids the world over do a lot of the same things, like snacking after school, riding bikes, flying kites, playing with each other, listening to music, hanging out. You may speak different languages and live oceans apart in very different kinds of homes, but still, when two kids meet, chances are you'll find something to share.

What many of us don't realize is that kids have always been pretty much the same— even kids from 5,000 years ago. Would you be surprised to know that the kids of old Egypt enjoyed swimming in the river, had favorite pets, and played

Leap Frog, Tug 'o War, and Senat, a game very much like checkers (see page 86)? Remember that favorite pull toy you had when you were just starting to walk? Well, believe it or not, kids in old Egypt played with the same kind of pull toy!

What do you think is meant by the expression "the more things change, the more they stay the same"?

EGYPTIANIZE YOURSELF

Yes, Egyptianize is a real word, meaning to use Egyptian styles, ideas, or customs. By creating some of the projects in this book you will be Egyptianizing yourself. You may even find it so interesting that you grow up to become an Egyptologist (pronounced E-gyp-TOL-o-gist). Egyptologists learn and teach about ancient Egypt. They usually work in museums, at universities, or at home, as writers. Or you may become an archaeologist who specializes in Egyptology!

If You Were a Child in Ancient Egypt

L et's step back in time. As a child whose family lives along the Nile thousands of years ago, your name would be made up of several words like "Welcome To You," "This Boy I Wanted," or "Our Girl Has Joined Us." Or, you might be named for a god, as in "Re Is Loving," or "Thoth Is Powerful."

Each morning, you'd wake up to the sun—not an alarm clock—and start the day with a prayer. And as you and your family take a moment to be thankful and grateful for the loving power of your god (the ancients prayed to many gods and goddesses, unlike most religions today), you know that all over Egypt, other people, rich and poor, are doing the same thing at this very same moment.

After prayers, you have a big breakfast — one that has to last you all day. (There is no lunchtime in ancient Egypt, only two large meals served at dawn and dusk.)

Running a little behind schedule? Don't worry about finding clean clothes to wear since it won't take you very long to get dressed. That's because the children of old Egypt didn't wear any clothes at all until they were teens!

WORK AND PLAY

In old Egypt, every day is "Take Your Child to Work Day." Each day, boys go with their fathers, and girls with their mothers, learning the jobs their parents do and helping them with their work. Only future scribes (writers) and doctors go to school as we know it. When payday comes, your parents receive baskets full of food and clothing from the people they work for. Your family doesn't miss having money, because there is no such thing!

What would you do at work with your parents? A boy might scatter seeds in the fields, build wooden boxes, give animals water, fix chariots, chisel stone, polish pottery, or pound papyrus

Think About It:

Kids running naked in the fields? A whole country praying every morning to many gods and goddesses? No lunch? Some things sure were different in ancient Egyptian times. But different doesn't mean better or worse. It is just, well, different. So why do you think that in today's world, people seem to feel uncomfortable around new or unusual or different ideas, religions, races—even different foods, clothing, and musical tastes? What could you do to help someone feel more comfortable about all the great things that make you different?

reeds (tall willowy water plants) into paper. And as they work, boys learn the songs the men sing to make their work more enjoyable.

A girl might carry water from the river, grind grain into flour, play with younger children, braid hair, make wigs, stir cosmetics, sew, or weave. Girls and women are often musicians and gymnasts, celebrating life through music and dance.

When harvest time comes, everyone helps in the fields. Girls toss corn high into the wind to clean it off. Boys bundle crops and put them inside baskets.

There is lots of work to do in old Egypt, but plenty of time for play, too. The ancient Egyptians love their children and encourage them to have plenty of fun. On the way back from watering the fields, you might stop for a swim in the clean water of the Nile River or one of its canals, play Tug 'o War, or leap frog your way home.

Leap Frog

To play Leap Frog, two people take turns. One crouches like a frog while the other jumps over her back, leaping like a frog before she, too, crouches down and gets leapt over. If you have four people, you can have a leap frog race in teams of two. Leaping frogs have lots of fun.

EGYPTIAN-STYLE Tug 'o War

For this game you need an even number of kids — at least four. Use chalk or a stick to make a line on the ground between teams. Then each team's players link elbows and tug, trying to pull the other team over the line. The team to pull the whole other team across the line wins.

In this game and all other children's games, the losers give the winners rides on their shoulders!

LIVING IN THE PALM OF NATURE

The kids of ancient Egypt spend most of their time outside, playing and working. Nature is yours for the having! As the sun rolls across the sky, you think of it as a most powerful god, blessing you with love, warmth, and life-giving power. You think of breezes as the breath of that great god.

You feel connected to the magic of nature, and every bird, animal, and insect has a special place in your wondrous world. You know that even a lowly beetle has amazing powers and can teach you about life.

Think About It:

Do you think that kids of today feel a closeness with nature? Were the kids of ancient Egypt able to commune with nature because it was part of their work and their play? If you could change something about your life, would it have anything to do with spending more time outdoors? To help you ponder these thoughts, go outside and say hello to all of nature. Maybe something will say hello back in its own special way.

Honoring the Beetle

Have you ever seen a scarab bracelet? The likeness of the beetle, or scarab, has been found on ornaments and jewelry since ancient times. The ancient Egyptians revered the scarab as a symbol of resurrection, or life after death.

You can make your own scarab. Find a large bar of soap, a dull butter knife, and a pencil. Draw a big beetle on the soap. Carve out the background, so that your beetle is raised from the soap bar. Display your scarab in your bathroom.

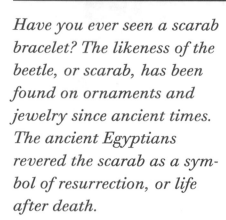

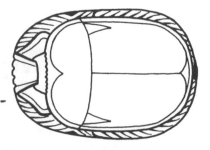

Think About It:

Many of the cures and rituals used by the doctors in old Egypt are still practiced today. Some American Indians speak to the spirits when a person is very sick. And many people use herbal medicines — very much like potions — to get well when they are sick. That's why we drink chamomile tea when we have an upset stomach or take a bath in cold tea to sooth a sunburn.

GOING TO THE DOCTOR

Today, when you go to the doctor, you go into a building where the doctor takes your temperature with a thermometer, examines you, and perhaps gives you medicine if you are sick.

But if you went to a doctor in ancient Egypt, the doctor's office would be in a temple, called The House of Life. The doctor would be somewhat like a doctor and somewhat like a priest. He would feel your head and then feel his own, so he could compare the temperatures. If you were sick, he would stand over you and chant a magical spell, speaking directly to your illness.

After chanting the spell, he might give you healing plants or potions to eat, too. Sometimes these concoctions smelled or tasted very bad. Ancient Egyptian doctors figured that awful medicine might make the illness want to leave the child's body!

Ancient Spell for a Stomach Bug

This ancient spell was used for a child with an infection in his stomach. Next time you or someone you know has a bellyache, you might want to give it a try.

> **Come out, you visitor of the darkness, who crawls along with your nose and face on the back of your head!**
>
> **Have you come to kiss this child? I forbid it!**
>
> **Have you come to hug this child? I forbid it!**
>
> **Have you come to take this child away? I forbid you to do so! I have made a potion to protect this child.**
>
> **I made it from garlic, which is bad for you but good for the child, and from honey, which is sweet for the living, but bad for you!**
>
> **Go now! And do not return!**

P. S. It's interesting that scientists of today have found that garlic and honey actually do kill some bad bacteria and help cure infections!

Make Up a Spell of Your Own

Try being an ancient Egyptian doctor yourself! Has your friend got a runny nose? Maybe smelling some vinegar or old socks will cure him! Has he got an earache? Perhaps playing some terrible music will make it go away. Make up the words of a spell to go along with your pretend cure.

THE FAMILY PET

Imagine having a little monkey as a pal who follows you around all day. Or, how about owning a fierce, protective goose who earns her keep by honking at strangers, chasing them away from your front yard? Maybe you have a trained cat or dog to go on long walks with you, catching a bird or two for dinner—or a goat to live in your yard and give you milk and cheese.

These were some of the pets people kept in ancient Egypt, and they were very much loved by the people who kept them, too.

Some pet owners kept the collar of their beloved pet, long after the pet had died. Then, when the person died, she'd have the collar buried with her, hoping to spend eternity with her favorite pet. (Some animals were treated like people and were even mummified when they died.)

Think About It:

Isn't it amazing that 5,000 years ago a young boy or girl, like you, had a cherished pet like you have (or want to have!) Ask about 15 people what kinds of pets they have and then make a bar graph to see which pet is most popular—cats, dogs, fish, birds, gerbils, hamsters, rabbits, or turtles.

NUMBER OWNED

KIND OF PETS

dogs cats birds fish turtles

Think About It:

How do you feel about homemade toys? Do they seem special to you because they are handmade, or do you see them as no good because they are not advertised on television? Do you think there is a difference between making someone a gift or buying a gift? Which would make you feel more special? Which would you enjoy playing with more?

Toys! Toys! Toys!

Balls, dolls, games, and little animal toys—we play with them today just as the children of ancient Egypt played thousands of years ago! Dolls were made of cloth and clay, play animals were made of wood or stone, and balls were made of linen rags wrapped around each other, tied with string, and painted.

There were no malls or big toy stores then, of course. Any plaything you owned would be a special one-of-a-kind toy, designed and made especially for you.

Pull Horse

Does this pull toy look familiar to you? People who study ancient Egypt actually found this wooden horse pull toy inside a royal tomb. It's pretty amazing to think that toddlers today still play with the exact same kind of toy when first starting to walk!

You can make a modern version from air-drying clay and two long nails. (If you don't have nails, use a bamboo skewer or two straight sticks— or even a pencil will do.)

In your hands, roll a hunk of clay into the shape of a large egg. Then pull out the horse's head, shaping the neck, face,

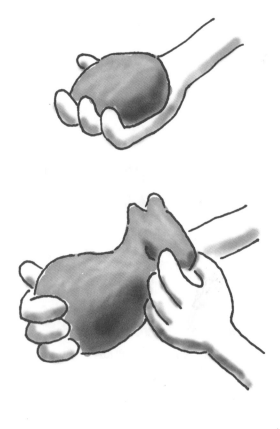

and ears. Then, pull out four legs, making the bottom of the legs thick enough to push the nails through. Remove the nails. Push a nail through the nose of the horse to make a hole for the pull string.

Use more clay to form four small, equal-sized circles for the wheels. Push each circle down like a fat hamburger, and pierce it in the middle with the nail.

Let the wheels and horse dry. When they are solid, push a nail through the front legs and wheel holes, and another nail through the back legs and wheel holes. Add a dab of fresh clay to the outside of the nails to hold the wheels in place. Push a string through the nose hole for pulling.

For a more modern update of this ancient toy, use two long screws and nuts to attach the wheels to the horse's legs.

Egyptian Lady or Goddess Doll

The ladies of old Egypt are famous for their beautiful hair, jewelry, and clothing designs. Goddesses like Isis (see page 50) were shown as beautiful ladies, too.

Use white air-drying or oven-drying clay to form a small Egyptian-style doll to hang on your wall, keep on your bureau, or give as a gift.

Form your figure with the legs and feet together and arms at her sides (if they're stretched out, they might break). For a standing doll, shape the base to look like a long, wide skirt and omit the legs and feet. Give the head a full shape, because Egyptian ladies often wore thick, braided wigs. (Make sure the neck is sturdy enough to

hold the head up.)

When the clay is dry, use fine-pointed markers to fill in the hair, eyes, lips, jewelry, and clothing. Make the hair and eyes black; the eyes should be large and dramatic. Use bright colors for the jewelry. You won't have to color in the dress, because in ancient Egypt women wore long white dresses.

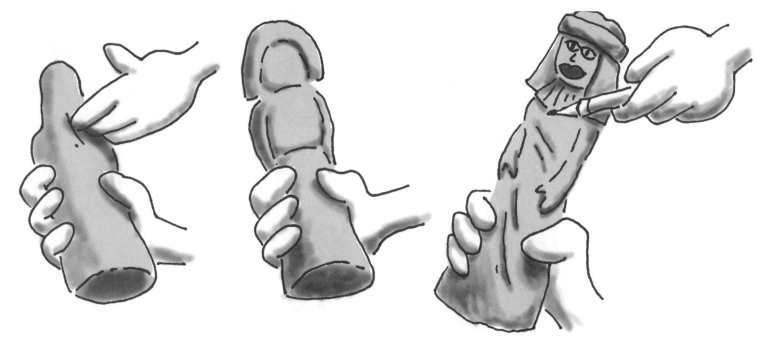

MORE ALIKE THAN DIFFERENT

You be the judge. Do you think kids today and kids from 5,000 years ago are more alike or more different? Make lists of all the similarities and differences. Are you glad to be alive now or do you think you might have preferred life in ancient Egypt?

The Ancients and the Power of Beliefs

Believe, believe, believe in magical forces of nature!
Believe with all your heart, mind, and soul!
Believe that you have a special place and play a special
part in this magical world!

That's the way it was long, long ago. To our distant ancestors, life was a magical experience, and the unseen hands of gods, goddesses, and nature worked miracles each and every day. They found power and wonder in everything, from stars to stones, from water to mathematics.

NEED A FAVOR? CALL ON THE LOCAL GOD

In our time, big cities have their own sports teams with local heroes. But in old Egypt each city had its hometown god or goddess. The people didn't exactly worship this god — that honor was saved for the powerful bringer of life, the god of gods, Amun-Re. Instead, people thought of the local god as someone to bargain with for favors.

If a farmer wanted good crops, or if a woman wanted to marry a certain man, she would bring a gift of food or clothing to the local temple and leave it with the priests to give to the local god or goddess. The priests took the offering and agreed to pray in the special language of the gods.

North, South, East, West

You may have to get up extra early to find out where north, south, east, and west are, but it's worth it! Knowing these directions connects you more powerfully to nature and will help you to experience the mystical side of ancient Egyptian culture.

Find a clear, paved area outside, like a driveway or sidewalk. Wake up at sunrise, get a piece of chalk, and go outside. Stand in the middle of the space, and draw a chalk circle around yourself. Now face the rising sun. Mark an "E" for east on that spot of the

Sun, Moon, and Stars

Instead of watching TV, the ancients watched the greatest "special" of all — the sky! Every corner of the sky — north, south, east, and west — belonged to gods and goddesses with mysterious, magical powers. The ancients placed their pyramids exactly in line with the four directions to take advantage of these magical sky powers.

circle. You're done for the moment. But don't forget to come back at noon to face the sun and make an "S" for south, and again at sunset to mark a "W" for west.

When you have the "E," "S", and "W" in place, put an "N" for north midway between east and west. You've made a homemade compass! It won't be exact, because the sun's position changes according to where you live and the time of year, but it will give you a rough idea of how to locate the four directions.

Another quick, but accurate way to find north: Look for moss on a tree trunk. It only grows on the north side! Once you've found north, here's how to find the other directions. As you face north, east will always be on your right and west on your left. South will be directly behind you.

That's a good thing to know if you are ever lost or trying to get someplace you've never been before.

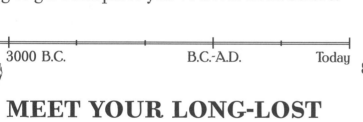

3000 B.C.　　　　B.C.-A.D.　　　Today

MEET YOUR LONG-LOST RELATIVES — BACK IN B.C.

Would you believe that the people who lived long ago were really your ancestors! They were the great, great, great, great, great, great and more great grandmothers and grandfathers of all of us who are alive today! They lived many generations ago.

A generation means all the people who are born at about the same date. You and your school friends are in the same generation, for instance. Your parents and their friends of the same age make up another generation, and so do your grandparents and friends their age. If you have children, they will be in yet another generation.

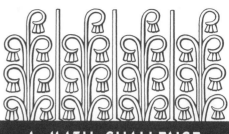

A MATH CHALLENGE:

HOW MANY GENERATIONS BACK WERE THE ANCIENT EGYPTIANS?

If ancient Egypt started about 5,000 years ago, and if it takes about 25 years for each generation to grow up and have children, then how many generations back were the ancient Egyptians? (Hint: Think division. See page 90 for answer.)

When you know the answer, you will also know how many "greats" to put in front of the words grandmother and grandfather. For fun, say all those greats out loud. This will give you a real experience of just how long ago ancient Egypt was!

Make a Time Line

A time line is a way to illustrate a sequence of events so that at a glance you can see clear relationships about when things happened. You can have a time line of a president's years in office, a time line of your grandparents' lives (a super surprise party birthday gift!), or a time line of any period in the history of the earth. Here is a time line of the ancient past, with some highlights of history marked on the line: You can make a time line of your life or your family history by making a line and marking

WHAT ARE B.C. AND A.D.?

When our calendar was invented, Christianity was not only a religion, it was the government, too. The people who started our calendar divided years into two time periods, the years before Christ was born and the years after Christ was born.

The years before Christ were written as B.C., and the years after Christ were written as A.D., which stands for "year of the lord" in Latin.

We now live in roughly 2000 A.D., but ancient Egypt started in 3000 B.C.—that's 5,000 years ago (2000 plus 3000).

it with events that are important to you.

Cut a poster in half (or thirds or fourths) the long way and tape the pieces end-to-end for a long, thin strip. Draw a line from end to end, the long way. Mark the line by years (short lines), going back to your beginning. Write in important dates. (If you're ten, you'll divide the line into ten equal spaces.) Over each mark, note the event you want to include. Add pictures or mementos.

CIRCUS

THE ANCIENT PAST IS NOW!

To the children of the distant future, you and your friends are living in the ancient past! To them, you and your experiences will be history! Isn't that a strange feeling?

What might people who live in the year 5000 A.D. – 3,000 years from now – know about the way you live today? Do you think they will truly understand your way of life? If an archaeologist (ark-ee-OL-o-gist) – someone who studies the ancient past – came to the place where you live 5,000 years from today, what would he or she find? The answers to these questions come from observations, thought, and imagination.

Look out your window now. If you see buildings, ask yourself, will they last for 5,000 years? Picture your hometown with all the wooden buildings gone (because wood does not usually last for thousands of years). What will the buildings that are left standing tell the people of the future? Do you think they will believe that our banks and office buildings are more important than people's homes?

One of the problems in learning about life in ancient Egypt is that the wooden buildings where people lived did not survive the passing of time. The buildings that lasted were stone temples and tombs like the pyramids. This gave historians the mistaken idea that the ancient Egyptians only thought about death and religion. But, fortunately, the Egyptians had writers, or scribes, and artists to tell a more complete story about life in old Egypt.

From their writings and drawings, as well as their pyramids, we learned that the people of ancient Egypt did think about life after death, but they gave more of their attention to love, work, health, food, music, dancing, games, and having fun!

Be a Future Archaeologist!

Think About It:

*T*he year is 4000 A.D. You have just arrived at the site of a dig—what archaeologists call their careful examination of sand and soil for relics of the past—and your supervisor wants to know what you have found and what conclusions you reach through your observations. What buildings do you see (remember this is about 2,000 years into the future)? What objects do you uncover from carefully sifting through the sand and soil? Does a story about life in this particular place begin to unfold from small pieces of pottery, decaying bones, or fossils pressed in rocks? What do you think the archaeologist will say about a golf ball, a ballpoint pen, an action figure, a miniature car, a plastic dinosaur?

You can go on a dig right in your yard. Just mark off a small area, called the site— preferably one with sandy or loose soil—and begin digging with a spoon. A shovel would be too big and you are interested in finding small things that will help you form a big picture (in your mind) of life long ago. Use a sifter to work through each layer of soil, putting aside any interesting objects you might find. Did you discover anything strange like a snail shell along a city walk? Bring your "finds" indoors and sit down with some friends to create a story about what you think might have happened at your site many years ago.

Long Ago in Egypt Land

No time period in history is perfect of course, but life in ancient Egypt may have come pretty close! While the people of ancient Europe were living in Stone Age conditions — on the edge of starvation, huddling in caves to escape the cold — the people of ancient Egypt were living it up, dressing in fine linen, partying on riverboats, and eating pastries. The common people of old Egypt each had a house and a little plot of land for growing food. What made life in old Egypt so much more advanced and comfortable?

Well, for starters, it hardly ever rains in Egypt, so most days are bright and sunny which helps make people happy. And the land was rich and fertile, too — good for growing food.

Every spring, the snow on Africa's Mountains of the Moon melted, spilling water into the Nile River and causing it to overflow. The Nile then flooded the surrounding land, leaving behind a thick layer of silt, or living black soil — the kind that is best for growing plants. People grew grains, like barley and corn, that could be stored, making Egypt a land with plenty for all.

Ancient Egypt was a safe land, too, free of invaders for most of its history. That's because it was surrounded by deserts that kept intruders out — and riches in.

The government of old Egypt was very stable, secure, and well-organized, too. The leaders—Egypt's royal pharaohs and the high priests—organized the society in a way that gave most people what they needed, and some people both what they needed and wanted. People who worked for the pharaoh or at the temple lived very well.

Think About It:

Do you think that people would be happy now if they were assured good weather, food, wise leaders, and peace among nations? Would that make the neighborhood you live in crime-free? What about greed (always wanting more)? Why do you think the Egyptians weren't greedy?

The common people worked hard, doing their part to make the society a good one. Their religion told them that if they were honest and responsible, they would enjoy the best that life had to offer. In the entire 3,000 years of ancient Egypt, there was little crime and few revolts.

With sunny weather, plentiful crops, wise leaders, and years of peace, it's no wonder ancient Egypt became the longest–lasting civilization known to history.

An UPSIDE-DOWN Land

When it comes to Egypt, up means down! Upper Egypt is actually in the lower (southern) part of the country. And Lower Egypt is the northern delta area, where the Nile River fans out to the Mediterranean Sea!

Even the Nile River is upside down! It is one of the few major rivers in the world that flows from south to north.

Until King Narmer (also known as Menes) united Upper Egypt and Lower Egypt, there were two lands—two separate tribes, with their own special gods and goddesses and special ways of life.

Narmer united the lands, but he wisely allowed the separateness and individual traditions of each Egypt to be respected. Every town or village

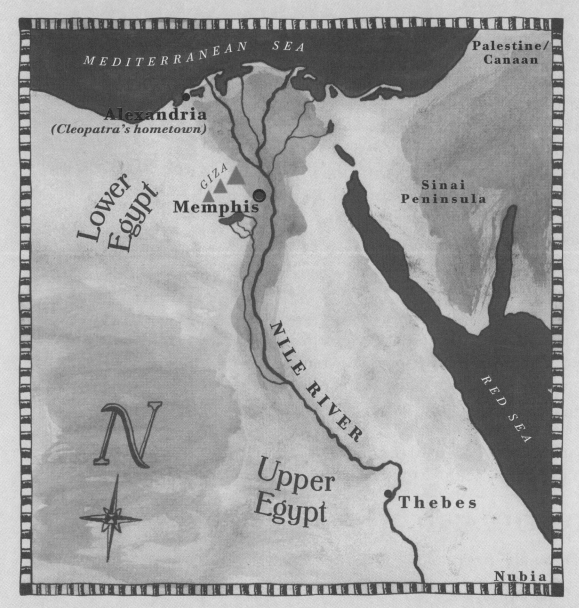

MEDITERRANEAN SEA

Palestine/
Canaan

Alexandria
(Cleopatra's hometown)

GIZA

Lower Egypt

Memphis

Sinai
Peninsula

NILE RIVER

N

RED SEA

Upper
Egypt

Thebes

Nubia

Think About It:

King Narmer certainly was a wise person, but a lot of credit goes to the Egyptians who wisely followed him. Why do you think the Egyptians lived so peacefully together? Do you think the people of today can live peacefully, too?

continued to celebrate its special god or goddess. (See page 21.)

Narmer made Memphis, where the two lands met, the capital. At important ceremonies, he – and all the pharaohs who came after him – wore the crowns of both Upper and Lower Egypt at the same time.

(They must have had strong necks!) Important ceremonies were always performed twice – once for Upper Egypt and once for Lower Egypt. (See pages 77-78 to make crowns.)

Even today, Egyptian people sometimes call their country "The Two Lands."

A LAND OF OPPOSITES

The idea of The Two Lands is a theme, or important idea in Egyptian history, and there are many other "twos." There are also the Red Land and the Black Land with the reddish sands of the Egyptian desert and the black fertile land along the Nile. There are actually places in Egypt where you can have one foot on fertile black farmland and the other on the sandy desert!

Another idea in the theme of The Two Lands is the life of people and the life of the gods. The pharaoh, as head of both the religion and government, was looked upon as the bridge that brought these separate realms together.

WHAT IS A SPHINX?

A sphinx is a large stone sculpture of a creature with a reclining body of a lion and the face of a human. They were built to remind the people of ancient Egypt that their rulers had extraordinary powers—the magical powers of both nature and the gods. The most famous sphinx is near the pyramids at Giza. Carved from natural desert rock, this sphinx seems to guard the pyramids that King Cheops and his family built so many years ago.

THE RIDDLE OF THE SPHINX

Here is a riddle that is thousands of years old:

**What walks on four legs in the morning,
two legs in the afternoon,
and three legs in the evening?**

Think hard and see what you and your friends come up with! You'll find the answer on page 90.

Think About It:

The yearly flooding of the Nile River made the farmland of old Egypt rich and fertile. But, in modern times, The Aswan High Dam was built to stop the flooding. This meant that new buildings could be constructed on land that was once flooded each year. But now the farmland of Egypt needs chemical fertilizers to make it good for growing.

Egypt was once a rich land. Now it is poorer. Do you think the dam was a good idea?

Create a Miniature Ancient Egypt

This project takes some time and patience, but imagine — at the end you'll have a whole country — supporting plant life, too!

YOU WILL NEED:

- large rectangular pan at least 3" (7.5 cm) deep (like a clean cat litter pan)
- map of Egypt (see page 29)
- sand
- potting soil
- small clay pyramids
- grass seed (or parakeet seed)
- strong foil
- rocks and pebbles
- small models of the pyramids and the sphinx, made from white air-drying clay or modeling clay (see page 45)
- grass, fresh or dry, to make small reed boats

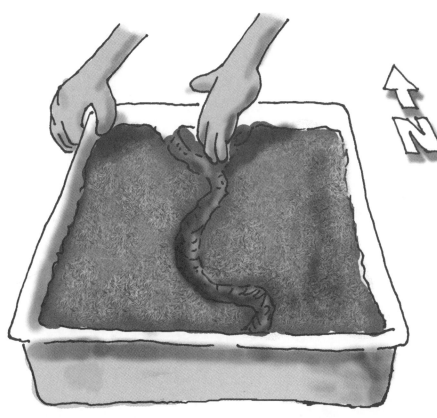

Place about 2" (5 cm) of soil on the bottom of the pan. Then look at the map of Egypt to see the snake–shaped Nile River winding through the middle of the country. Press the soil down or push it away from where the river bed and its two main delta branches (the Rosetta Branch and the Damietta Branch) will be.

To make the Nile River bed, use strong or doubled–up foil to form a curved foil version of

CONTINUED ➤

the river and its delta. Use extra foil at both ends so that you have a piece to fold over the ends of the pan to keep the river self-contained.

Cut the foil into a "Y" shape to make the Rosetta Branch and the Damietta Branch.

Gently press the foil riverbed down into the soil. (If some soil falls into the river, that's okay.) Put a few smooth pebbles in the river to weight it down.

Cover the long sides of the pan with a thick layer of sand. Fill in the area on both sides of

the river and inside the delta with soil.

Add larger rocks to the right side of the pan, as mountains. Press the seeds into the potting soil alongside the river and in the delta.

Fill the river with water.

To water your Egypt:

Water your model of ancient Egypt the way Mother Nature used to do it. Once a week, pour extra water into the foil riverbed so it overflows its banks (sides) and floods the land (potting soil) where the seed has been planted.

When the grass seed sprouts, you will see lush green life near the river. That's the way it was in ancient times. (With weekly watering, your land of Egypt will last for two or three months.)

Add the pyramids:

On the map, notice that the pyramids are all on the west side of the river. That's the side where the sun sets.

The ancient Egyptians believed that Amun-Re, the Sun God, went west every evening to enjoy eternal life. They wanted to go west after they died to be with him.

Map markers:

For fun, add markers naming the nearby lands or features of the ancient world. Snip paper triangles, like miniature baseball pennants, write the names of the neighboring lands or bodies of water, and attach them to toothpicks.

(Wind the paper around the wood once before attaching.)

Nubia, the lush African land, is south. To the north is the Mediterranean Sea, where sailors took off for Syria and Phoenicia to trade. To the west is the Red Sea, and to the east is Libya.

P.S. *For a super–duper Land of Egypt, get permission (and help) to create an outdoor Egypt in an old sandbox or child's wading pool.*

THE RIVER NILE: A WATERY HIGHWAY

Move over, modern superhighway; make room for the most super highway of all – the Nile River. The Nile was fully automated, or so it seemed! When a boat traveled north, the river's currents carried it north. And when boats went south, the winds filled the boat's sails and pushed it southward.

The simplest boats were giant papyrus reeds tied together. (These tall reeds were also used to make the Egyptian version of paper. In fact, that's where the word paper comes from!)

The royal class—the Pharaoh, his family, their court, and the priests—had wooden boats, made with cedar wood from Syria. Oarsmen chanted songs and prayers as they rowed.

Think About It:

How do you think people made maps and captured the idea of Egypt as lotus shaped if there were no airplanes 5,000 years ago for an aerial view?

EGYPT: A LOTUS FLOWER LAND

When people went to parties in ancient Egypt, they were each given a lotus flower to hold. Look on the map of Egypt and you will see why. The fertile part of the country where people can live, *near the S-shaped Nile River, looks like a lotus blossom on a long, floating stem.*

Look at a map of the place where YOU live. What shape or symbol can you find in it?

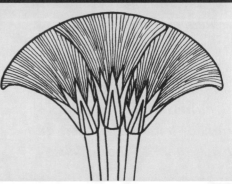

Make Reed Boats

You can make a miniature model of the Egyptian grass boats. Cut about 6"– 8" (15–20 cm) of fresh or dried grass and tie it with string near each end, leaving space at the end. Snip the ends into a point. Bend the grass and gently stretch it outward in the middle to make a hammock shape. Your boat will float and look like the reed boats of long, long ago.

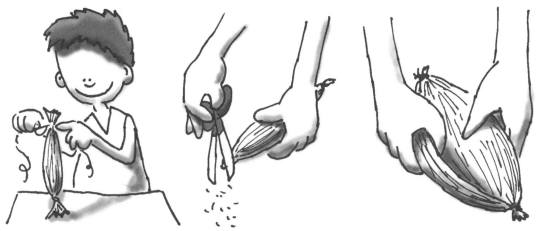

THE BUSINESS OF BARTER

Waterways were the highways of the world for many years. Ports along the oceans and ports along the rivers (called inland waterways) kept traders in business. Traders in ports would bargain and barter their products, perhaps trading coffee beans for wheat, or furs for grain.

Here's a game to play with one or more players. The first player looks at a globe or a world map and tells:

> ▹ where he is
> ▹ what route he will take to his next port
> ▹ where he will land

The first person to say what that player has in his ship and what he will find in his new port, gets to be it. Now she names her present port, route, and where she will land. And so on until you've traveled up and down the world's waterways, buying and selling the natural products of the earth. Although this is a game, it is not far from how things evolved over the centuries.

A BATHTUB NILE

Your bathtub can be the Nile with north-ward water currents and your breath as the southerly wind currents.

Fill the bathtub half-way, and let the water settle until it is smooth and calm. Then gently blow on it from one end of the tub, like a gentle southern wind. Your breath is like the wind that would push sail-boats south.

To make the currents take the boats in a northerly direction, gently dip one hand into the tub and push the water in one direction only. When you see the water moving, send your reed boat along on the currents.

If there are two of you boating, you can launch several boats at once.

Superstars of Old Egypt

Five thousand years can produce a lot of great people, and naturally there's not enough room to tell about them all here. Here are seven superstars for our Old Egypt Hall of Fame.

AKHENATEN   NEFERTITI

King Narmer (or Menes)

Little is known about the man who united Upper and Lower Egypt, but he must have been quite a guy. He ended the fighting of many tribes, made peace, and created the kingdom of ancient Egypt. The government he started was so stable and secure that it continued for thousands of years! (See page 28.)

Akhenaten and Nefertiti

King Akhenaten and his wife, Queen Nefertiti, were superstars who changed the way people thought and acted. Akhenaten took two years to build a city to honor Aten, his sun god. The city had fabulous palaces, open-roofed temples, lush gardens, and wide roadways. Here the common people had more power and respect than anywhere else in ancient Egypt. Akhenaten believed that since Aten shone down on everyone equally, everyone had equal worth. He encouraged people to see the royal family not as gods, but as good and noble people who knew how to enjoy life.

Alas, his beautiful dream for society faded because the army and the priests of the other gods were angered by his neglect of them. They joined together against Akhenaten. The gentle king and his wife disappeared into history, as did his splendid city.

TUTANKHAMEN

Tutankhamen married Akhenaten's daughter and became the next pharaoh of Egypt. No one knows exactly why or how he died at the age of about 21, but some archaeologists think he may have been murdered!

King Tut's claim to fame in our time, however, is that his tomb is the only one that had not been robbed of its royal treasures. You can see Tut's possessions today in the Egyptian Museum in Cairo.

Think About It:

Here we see that everything was fine in old Egypt as long as people accepted their roles in life. As soon as the balance changed between people and royalty, thereby diminishing the role of the high priests, trouble began to brew. Are you surprised by this?

IMHOTEP

This brilliant man designed the world's first pyramid, King Zoser's step pyramid at Saqqara (see page 47). Imhotep helped Zoser organize the country. He was also the world's first known scientist and doctor, as well as a priest and a famous writer!

After he died, people began to think of him as a god — the god of medicine and healing. But being worshipped probably would have displeased Imhotep, for he was one of the earliest believers in one powerful god — the sun god — rather than believing in many gods and goddesses.

QUEEN HATSHEPSUT
(HOT-SHEP-SOOT)

Like other Egyptian pharaohs, Queen Hatshepsut was considered a living goddess during her reign. She sent a fleet of trading ships to the mysterious Land of Punt loaded with fruit, meat, and colorful beads. These ships

brought back spectacular treasures, including plenty of gold. (Hatshepsut even had sandals of pure gold!)

This strong, but gentle leader ruled for 22 years, bringing good times to the people of Egypt, making Hatshepsut one of the best-loved pharaohs.

CLEOPATRA

The charm and beauty of this lady, one of the last of the Egyptian royals, have been praised for ages. (Shakespeare, the great English playwright, even wrote a play about her.)

In Cleopatra's day, the Romans were claiming Egypt for their own. But that didn't seem to stop her from enjoying life. History tells us that Cleopatra was a flirt! According to one story, she had herself rolled up in a carpet and delivered to Julius Caesar, the Roman leader who had come to rule Egypt. He must have been surprised to see the beautiful queen being unrolled at his feet when he moved into his new headquarters! He supposedly fell in love with her on the spot.

Very recently, Cleopatra's palace was discovered underwater in the harbor of the city of Alexandria. The huge stone pillars still proclaim her glory.

Surfing through time: Visit King Zoser on the Net

King Zoser may be long gone, but he lives on as an internet site. Check out this site for an interesting look at his tomb and temple.

http://ccat.sas.upenn.edu/arth/zoser/zoser.html

THE PYRAMIDS AT GIZA: WONDERS OF THE ANCIENT WORLD

The Great Pyramid of Giza, Egypt – one of four that still remain there – is the grandest pyramid of all. It's so large that it can be seen from the moon! It's also the oldest structure on the face of the earth, built about 4,600 years ago. Picture 33 one–story houses standing on top of each other, and you will have an idea of how high the Great Pyramid stands!

Built by King Khufu (also called Cheops), the Great Pyramid and the three smaller pyramids that stand near it are the only one of the seven wonders of the ancient world that still exists. When the Great Pyramid was first built, it was covered with bright, white limestone and had tips of solid gold. And think about this – the 2,500,000 stones used to make it were cut so perfectly that the thinnest piece of paper can't be slipped between the stones even today. That's almost unbelievable!

HOUSES OF ETERNAL LIFE

The ancient Egyptians called pyramids "Houses of Eternal Life." They believed that if a pharaoh's body could be preserved (mummified) after death, the pharaoh had a good chance at living forever as long as he had been a good person. If the pharaoh lived forever, he or

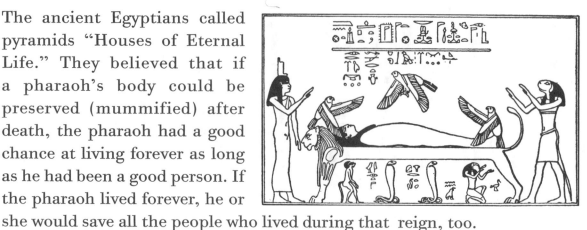

she would save all the people who lived during that reign, too.

To ancient Egyptians, heaven would be just like everyday life, but with no problems. In heaven, you would still need food, friends, and furniture, just as you did in regular life. That is why the pyramids were filled with the pharaoh's earthly treasures.

King Khufu's body and treasures were never found in the Great Pyramid at Giza. Grave robbers of long, long ago found their way in and took the treasures.

Pyramid Fun Facts

Pyramids were connected to other buildings by a very long tunnel (longer than three football fields set end-to-end). That's so the priests could visit the tomb to pray and leave fresh food for the dead person.

Other buildings near the pyramids were temples, libraries, schools, and storage places, a kind of ancient downtown where people actually traded goods and services. In that sense, the pyramids were as much a place for the living as they were for the dead.

The temples and palaces had extremely high ceilings, which they painted on top to look like colorful bundles of papyrus. These pillars were much higher than any ladder could go. How do you think the clever Egyptians got high up to paint them? (For the answer, see page 90.)

Think About It:

Different religions have different beliefs about life after death, heaven, and the rewards for living a good life. Talk about what you believe is important in life and in death with your friends and family.

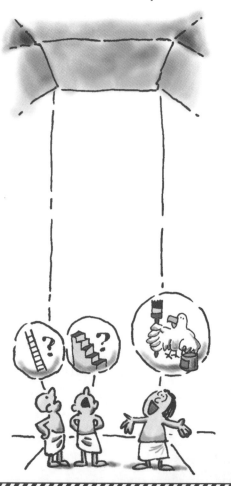

SLAVES BUILT THE PYRAMIDS — NOT!

Because so much time has gone by, we cannot know every little fact about ancient Egyptian life. But one thing is certain: The pyramids were NOT built by slaves.

The men who constructed the pyramids were farmers who could not farm during the three months a year when the Nile River overflowed (see page 30). They were paid for their labors with housing, food, and clothing for themselves and their families.

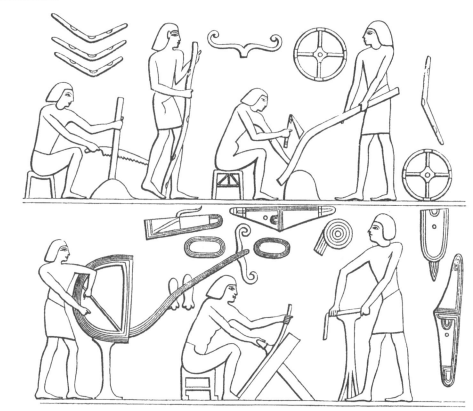

A Math Teaser

It's said that King Khufu hired 100,000 men to build The Great Pyramid. The men worked 3 months a year for 20 years. If the men had worked all year long, without stopping, how many years would it have taken to build the Great Pyramid? (For the answer, see page 90.)

Think About It:

If the pyramids were being built in a freezing northern climate, how might the stone have been cut? There is one stone that is harder than any others, so it is used to cut stones. Do you know which stone that is?

Cutting the Stones

Cutting massive blocks of stone is not easy, but the clever Egyptians found a way to do it. They would chisel holes into large stones with copper tools and then insert pieces of dry wood into the holes. Then they would water the wood. When the wood expanded, the stone broke into pieces.

NO ELEVATORS BACK THEN

How did the pyramid builders get the stones to the top of the pyramid? There were no elevators back then — pulleys and elevators had not yet been invented!

The clever Egyptians built mud ramps around the construction and pulled the stones up on log sledges. Each massive stone had been cut so carefully that it would slide into place perfectly.

Watch a Pyramid Video

Public Television offers an interesting video exploring the construction of the Great Pyramid at Giza. Ask your school librarian if it is in the library or a classroom. (To order it, call 1-800-828-4PBS. It costs money so please get permission first.)

Make a sledge:

A sledge is a simple machine used for moving objects. To test out whether sledges work, first try moving a heavy book by giving it a gentle nudge with your nose, or your pinky finger. (Pushing with your hand would be too easy!)

Next, put five round pencils on a table top, spaced about 2" (5 cm) apart, and place the book on top. Try moving the book with the pencil sledge. What a difference!

The American-Egyptian Connection

During the last half of the Egyptian empire, far across the ocean, in the land that is now Central and South America, other pyramids were being constructed by the Aztec, Maya, Olmec, Inca, and other peoples. Their pyramids, too, were majestic. They, too, worshipped a powerful sun god and decorated their walls with hieroglyphs. (See pages 58-62.)

Can all these similarities be coincidence, something that happened at random? Or were the people of the ancient American cultures somehow connected to the ancient Egyptians?

Many — in fact, most — scholars believe the American pyramid-building peoples had no connection to the ancient Egyptians. They say the languages of each were too different for the cultures to be related.

Thor Heyerdahl is a Norwegian who set out to prove that ancient Egyptians could have sailed across the ocean to America. In 1969, he and his crew set out from Egypt in papyrus boats — the kind the ancient Egyptians used for most of their water travel.

Sure enough, he arrived in South America, convincing some people that the two cultures might be connected after all! What do you make of this?

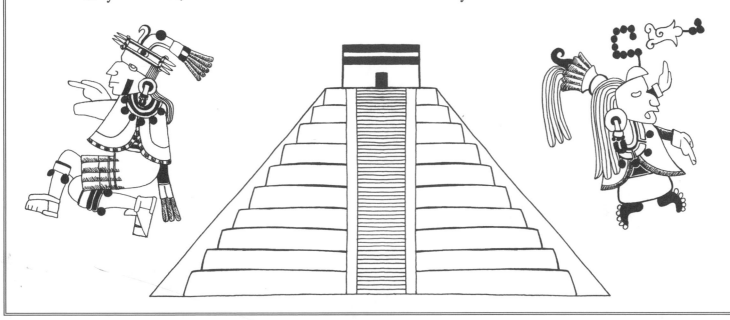

PYRAMIDS GALORE!

The pyramid shape, and pictures of the pyramids, are all around you. You can find pyramids on business signs, travel brochures, on TV, and in books and magazines, too.

VISIT A MODERN PYRAMID

Moody Gardens in Galveston Island, Texas, is a one–acre garden inside a beautiful glass pyramid. When you visit this pyramid, you also get to visit a rain forest.

The Louvre Museum in Paris has a pyramid entrance that was designed by I.M. Pei, one of the great architects of our time. While you're in France, the botanic garden in the city of Nice has a giant pyramid greenhouse.

City Club Vienna Hotel has a glass pyramid that contains a pool, sports center, and restaurant that's open to the public.

Summon Pyramid in Salt Lake City is a small pyramid that was built as a winery in 1979.

One of the biggest modern American pyramids is **The Great American Pyramid** in Memphis, Tennessee. It's a sports and entertainment arena that stands 321 feet (96.3 m) high and covers almost seven acres!

Last but not least, the world's fourth largest pyramid is in Las Vegas, Nevada. It was so shiny in the sun that airplane pilots complained and the shine was toned down!

Go On A Pyramid Hunt:

Do you think you will see pyramids three times today? You just might, if you go on a pyramid hunt! Here's a hint to get you started: Look at a U.S. one dollar bill.

Create Clay Pyramids

White air-drying clay can be shaped into excellent miniature pyramids. The trick is to form the base into a perfect square with four triangular walls coming up from it to meet in a point at the top.

To make the pyramid, press out the clay like cookie dough into four triangles and one square. Make the base of the triangles the same length as the sides of the square.

Place the base of each of the triangles onto the square and join them at the top. Press the seams of the walls together gently. To make your pyramids as dazzling as the pyramids of ancient times, dip the tip into glue and then into gold glitter.

Think About It:

When you make your clay pyramid, you can also form equal-sized creations in other shapes, like a square, a rectangle, or a round sphere.

When all these objects, including your pyramid, are dry, line them up on a tabletop. Use your breath to try to blow them down. Which shape stays in place the longest?

Wobble the tabletop like an earthquake. What is the most stable shape? Look back to page 25 to see how the most stable shape can influence what archaeologists conclude as we look back and think forward.

Construct a Cardboard Pyramid

You'll need tape, scissors, and cardboard. (Decorate the cardboard before you tape the structure together.)

Constructing a simple cardboard pyramid will not take 20 years, of course, but it will give you an idea of the magic of geometry, the branch of math that deals with shapes. (In geometry, the pyramid shape is called a polygon, meaning a structure with many sides.)

To make a 10" (25 cm) pyramid, cut a 10"-square base from cardboard. Then cut four triangles that are 10" on the bottom and have two equal sides.

Loosely tape the sides together on the inside and stand them up to form the pyramid. Glue the pyramid to its base with white glue.

A gleaming pyramid: To make your cardboard pyramid gleam like the limestone pyramids of ancient times, paint the cardboard with white tempera paint before you tape the structure together, and give the tip the glitter treatment: Paint the tip with glue and then shake gold glitter on.

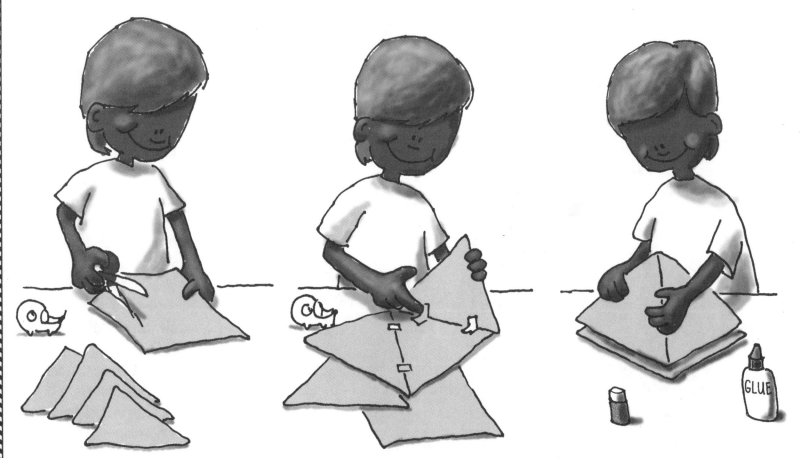

Pyramid Basics

Any of the pyramids described here will work well in your Land of Egypt (see page 31). Or, you can expand on these ideas using materials you have handy. The basic premise of pyramid construction is that the base of each of the four triangles must be equal to the side of the square. If you follow that rule, you can build miniature pyramids and huge super pyramids for camping outdoors.

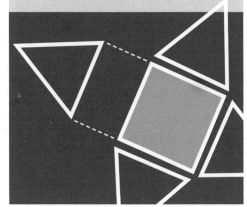

Make a Block or Can Pyramid

Creating a pyramid with cans or blocks is more of a challenge than you might think. (Remember to start with a square on the bottom.)

If your blocks are long gone, try using recycled cereal boxes or recycling cans to make a pyramid. (You can gradually add to the base and the height as you collect cans, blocks, or boxes.)

Try a Lego or Block Step-Pyramid

The very first pyramid was a step pyramid built by King Zoser of Egypt. Later Egyptian pyramid builders eliminated the steps.

Try creating a six-step pyramid from Legos or other building blocks. Remember, the pyramid needs to start on a square base.

PYRAMID POWER: IS IT REAL?

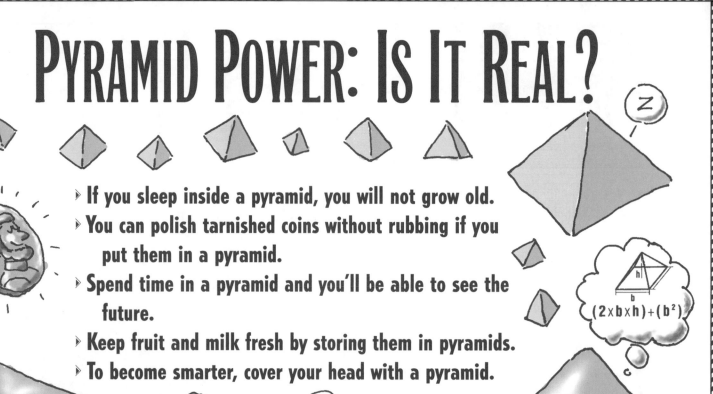

- If you sleep inside a pyramid, you will not grow old.
- You can polish tarnished coins without rubbing if you put them in a pyramid.
- Spend time in a pyramid and you'll be able to see the future.
- Keep fruit and milk fresh by storing them in pyramids.
- To become smarter, cover your head with a pyramid.

$(2 \times b \times h) + (b^2)$

Ideas about the magical powers of the pyramid have been around for years. Supposedly, a dentist in California keeps a pyramid hanging from the ceiling over his patients' heads. He believes that his patients get fewer cavities and heal faster because of it!

Once, a young man decided to camp out inside an ancient pyramid. He thought sleeping there would make him smarter. That night, he felt as if he couldn't breathe. Then, colored lights appeared before his eyes, and a "strange energy" seemed to enter his body. When he left, he felt very peaceful and said he felt he knew all there was to know.

Hmm.... What do you think about his experience with pyramid power?

Test for pyramid power: To see if pyramid power may be something real, try placing one slice of raw fruit under a pyramid that you made and another equal-sized slice under a rectangle or square (like a shoe box). Which keeps the fruit fresh longer?

ART IN ANCIENT EGYPT

Painted scenes on the pyramid walls show the ancients as calm, cheerful people living life to the fullest. The faces on the statues have peaceful smiles. Husbands and wives, sisters and brothers, sit side-by-side, their hands resting on each other's shoulders, or arms around each other's waists. Their stone faces are alert and satisfied.

No wonder the life-loving Egyptians believed in an afterlife that was just like the life they lived. They didn't want to stop living – ever!

THE FIRST MOTION PICTURES

The pictures on pyramid walls are like the very first movies, because they show the action of life, telling a story as they go. Ancient Egyptians painted scenes, one after the other, of people having fun, working, and worshipping. Musicians sing and play. Dancers dance. People give gifts. Kids leap frog, and workers cut the harvest. Cattle graze, and monkeys help people by picking figs off a tree.

To the ancients in Egypt, art was a kind of magical message to the gods, like a painted prayer. Artwork from those days featured part-human, part-animal gods and goddesses, too. These other-worldly creatures are shown in scenes of everyday life, protecting, guiding, and adding magic to the everyday world.

Create an Egyptian Statue

Use air–drying or oven–baking clay to form a statue in the style of the ancients. Egyptian statues show people sitting or standing. Their arms were usually on their knees or at their sides. They were dressed as they would be in life (see pages 81-83). Parents were made very large and children very small.

Many Gods and Goddesses

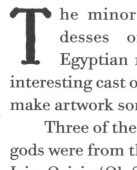

OSIRIS

The minor gods and goddesses of the ancient Egyptian religion were an interesting cast of characters who make artwork something special.

Three of the most important gods were from the holy family of Isis, Osiris (Oh-SI-ris), and their son, Horus.

The women and girls of ancient Egypt tried to be as wise and loving as Isis, the mother of the family. Men made the strong and protective father, Osiris, their hero. Boys looked up to Horus, the loyal son who helped his parents.

The walls of the pyramids and temples are full of pictures of this special family. Isis is drawn as a beautiful and graceful woman. But Horus is often drawn with the head of a falcon. (Falcons are good hunters that can

ISIS

HORUS

travel very fast, and Horus was believed to have these traits.)

Osiris, the king of the afterlife, was often shown with the face of the reigning pharaoh. That was one way to communicate to the people that the pharaoh had the powers of a god.

Draw Like an Ancient Egyptian

The distinctive drawing style of ancient Egypt has been preserved all these years, telling us stories of relationships, what is important, what people did, and what they believed. Here are some tips to follow if you want to draw like an ancient Egyptian artist:

▶ *Draw the head, eyes, legs, and feet as if you were looking at them from the side. But draw the body as if looking at it from the front.*

▶ *Don't use depth or perspective. If you want to show distance, put the thing that's far away on the top or bottom of the picture. Make the most important person or creature larger than others in the drawing.*

▶ *Show a scene in which something is happening.*

▶ *Draw women in light colors and men in dark colors. (Men probably were more tan because they worked outside, while women were more often indoors, out of the sun.)*

Make a Wall Painting

You will need several sheets of paper (butcher paper or connected computer paper work very well) and art materials such as markers, chalk pastels, or colored pencils.

Here is one way to approach a wall painting. Think of an activity you like, such as playing ball, dancing, or gardening. If you decide to draw the story of your life, show a scene of your parents, then draw them with a small baby. Next, show a small child, and then draw a scene with you as you are today, doing something you like to do.

If you are having fun, don't stop there! What else do you think will happen in your life? What would you like to happen? Draw it all, Egyptian-style.

Think About It:

Look at some artwork in art books by well-known artists from your country such as Whistler, Winslow Homer, Edward Hopper, and Mary Cassatt from America. How do they reveal perspective (near and far), depth, three dimensions, age, size, and relationships in their art?

WHAT TO DRAW?

What to draw is up to you, of course. You may choose to draw in the ancient Egyptian style choosing subjects from your life today. You can tell a story, express your beliefs, and what is important to you much as Egyptian artists did. Or, you may choose to stay in the past for both your subjects and your techniques. Leaf through this book to get some ideas and don't be hesitant about tracing some images to help you get the feeling for this artistic style.

Remember, if you are doing a frieze (see page 54), keep your plaster drawing simple. Draw the outline as if you were creating the black lines of a coloring book in the plaster.

Egyptian Symbols

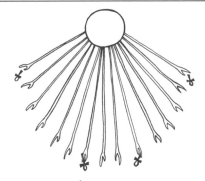

THE ANKH: ▷
This represented the power of the sun god. Ancient Egyptians believed that carrying it or wearing it brought good luck.

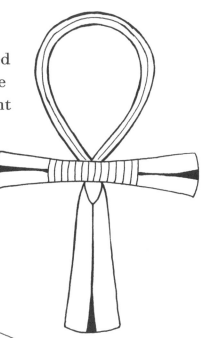

KEPHRI: In real life, this scarab beetle pushes a little ball of dirt along the ground. To the ancient Egyptians, he stood for the way life started, with the ball of the sun being pushed into the world. (See page 14 for more on scarabs.) ▽

ATEN: This was one way of drawing the sun god. Its little hands and ankhs bring life to everyone.

◁ **ANUBIS:** The jackal-headed Anubis helps people move into the afterlife when they first die.

TAWERET: ▷
This standing goddess, with her hippopotamus head, lion limbs, and big belly was thought to be a fierce protector of pregnant women and babies.

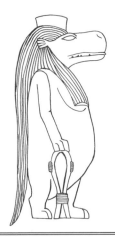

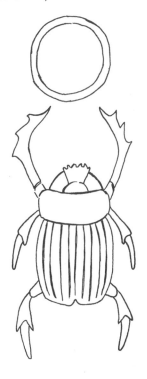

APOPHIS: This fancy snake was thought to eat up the sun when it disappeared every evening.

Make a Frieze, or Plaster Relief

T he walls of pyramids sometimes had art chiseled into them, or art with the backgrounds chiseled out. These 3-D scenes are called reliefs or friezes. A plaster relief will probably take more than one day to complete, but just think, in the end you will have a lasting work of art. We are still enjoying ancient Egyptian friezes after 5,000 years!

YOU WILL NEED:

▹ **shoe box lid (or bottom of a large milk carton)**
▹ **no—stick cooking oil**
▹ **plaster and water**
▹ **white vinegar (optional)**
▹ **sandpaper**
▹ **sculpting tool (nail, old metal nail file, or other tool)**
▹ **tempera, poster, or watercolor paints**

Spray the inside of the shoe box lid with no—stick cooking oil. In a bowl, mix the plaster and water according to the directions on the package, or 2 parts water to 1 part plaster. (A dash of white vinegar slows the hardening process.)

Pour the plaster into the lid, right up to the top. (The thicker your frieze, the less likely it is to break.) The perfect time to sculpt is when the plaster is almost hard, but still damp. You'll notice that plaster loses its shine as it hardens. (Dry plaster works, too; it's just not quite as easy to work with.)

Sculpt by drawing the out-line of a picture with a sculpt-ing tool like a nail. It's like drawing the outlines in a color-ing book that you'll color later. Sand around the outline of the pictures to make the subject stand out. (You can swab any little lumps of plaster, or sand them when the relief is dry.) Add hieroglyphs around the edge (ancient Egyptian sym-bols, see page 53).

Paint before you remove from the box.

CONTINUED ➤

MILK CARTON FRIEZE

A smaller relief can be made in the bottom of a waxed half-gallon (half-liter) milk carton. Cut off the bottom 3" (7.5 cm) and rinse out the carton. Mix $^2/_3$ cup (150 ml) plaster with $^1/_3$ cup (75 ml) water, right in the carton, and let the plaster begin to dry. When it has lost its shine, draw your picture with a long nail or metal file.

When the plaster dries, remove from the carton. Turn it over and you may find a surprise on the underside. There may be pyramids there just waiting for you to fill in for an interesting pyramid scene!

COLORING THE RELIEF

To "age" your relief, coat it with light tan or orange watercolor paint, or even a coat of strong tea. If you wish to add color to your relief, let the aging coat dry completely (overnight is best) before you fill in with colors.

Use bright colors, deep watercolors, even gold or copper paint to fill in your subject. Paint red crowns, jet black hair, bright blue jewelry, rich green plants. Aha! You've discovered ancient treasure (one you made yourself!).

A Pop-Up Pyramid with a Pop-Out Pharaoh

Of course, pop-up cards weren't part of the technique of the ancients. Here, we are borrowing some ideas and symbols from the ancients and applying them in a new, modern way. Combining the very old with the new in this way makes a good gift, a special card, or an interesting display. The front shows the pyramids at Giza, under a bright moon or sun. When the card is opened, a pharaoh pops out, sitting on his or her throne.

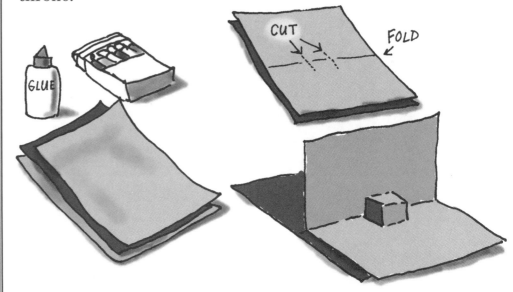

 YOU WILL NEED:

» **3 pieces of stiff paper**
» **glue**
» **drawing materials (colored pencils, pens, markers)**

Line up two pieces of paper and fold them in the center. Take one of the pieces and make two cuts about 1" (2.5 cm) deep in the center. Push the fold of the center cut out so it forms a pop-out square.

Now you are ready to decorate the paper with the pop-out square as the palace. The top of

the paper will become the walls; the bottom half of the paper will become the floor, or garden. (Remember that the pharaoh will be attached to the pop-out, so leave room for him.)

When the inside is decorated, glue the two pieces of paper together with the pop-out piece on the inside of the fold.

Trace or draw a pharaoh on a throne on the third sheet of paper. Cut him out and glue him to the pop-out, as if he were sitting.

Draw and cut out a pyramid and a glowing sun or full moon for the cover of the card.

Attach the pyramid and the sun or moon with a little piece of paper folded in a zigzag. (Three or four folds are enough.)

Glue the bottom of the zigzag to the front of the card where you want objects to pop up. Glue the top of the zigzag to the back of the pyramid and to the sun or moon, and attach.

HIEROGLYPHICS: WRITING IN PICTURES

The little drawings that made up the written Egyptian language are called hieroglyphs (HI-row-glifs). In the earliest days of ancient Egypt, these pictures were used to show what the scribe, or writer, wanted to communicate. A picture of a foot, for instance, might have stood for the word walking. A picture of a boat might have stood for the word travel.

But using pictures for writing can be confusing. A foot could also mean kicking, or dancing, or simply, a foot. As time went by, the pictures came to stand for certain sounds instead of whole words. That way, the Egyptians could spell out words, much as we do today.

Can you guess what these hieroglyphics once stood for?

Can you decode this hieroglyphic message? See page 90 for the answers.

HAIL, SCRIBE!

Not many people could read or write back in the time of the ancients. Only special people called scribes had that ability. Usually, scribes were the sons of powerful people of Egypt. They attended school for long hours each day to learn their profession. Their parents knew that once a person could read and write, he would have an honored job for life.

Scribes kept records and assisted the royal family and high priests in running the nation.

Learning to write the 750 hieroglyph signs must have been a lot like learning four- and five-digit long division without a calculator! The rules of the written language were difficult to master. To make learning more interesting, teachers created practice sentences that poked fun at the other occupations and told how great it was to be a scribe.

Here is the fine charioteer, so proud of his chariot! But when the wheel breaks off, his horse splatters him with mud. Be a scribe and you will have no mud on your face!

Think About It:

The English alphabet has only 26 letters, and although some letters like "C" have both hard and soft sounds, the alphabet isn't too difficult to learn. Find out how many letter symbols there are in the Greek alphabet, the Japanese alphabet, the Chinese alphabet, and the Russian alphabet. Whew!

Egyptian Numbers

Here is a chart showing numbers as the ancient Egyptians wrote them.

They used the same digit for 1 to 9, writing it over and over for larger numbers. How would you write the year you were born? (Remember that dates such as 1981 mean in the year one thousand nine hundred eighty-one.)

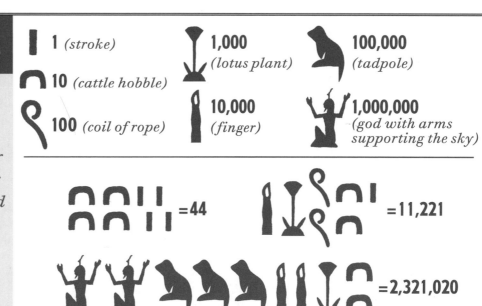

1 *(stroke)*

10 *(cattle hobble)*

100 *(coil of rope)*

1,000 *(lotus plant)*

10,000 *(finger)*

100,000 *(tadpole)*

1,000,000 *(god with arms supporting the sky)*

= 44

= 11,221

= 2,321,020

The Hieroglyphic Alphabet

Use this portion of the hieroglyphic alphabet that corresponds to the letter sounds of the English alphabet to write your name and to send secret messages.

Hieroglyph		Sound
A [vulture]		at, Alan, Ariel, hat
[forearm]		make, Jason
B [foot]		Bill, boy, bike
C [basket] / [hillside]		Clayton, cover, Carmon
[folded cloth]		Cynthia, spice, cent
CH [hobble rope]		change, Charles
D [hand]		do, dine, Dana
E [two reed leaves]		seed, Ethan
[vulture]		early, pet, Erin,
F [horned viper]		fair, Frank, Farrell
G [pot stand]		girl, Greg, Greta
[cobra]		giraffe, Jane, George
H [shelter] or [rope]		help, house, Henry, Howard, Jose,

Hieroglyph		Sound
I [reed leaf]		sit, sight, Iris, Irene
J [cobra]		jelly, Jane, Jim
K [basket] or [hillside]		kite, kick, Kate
L [open mouth]		live, Larry, Lori
M [owl]		mum, Mom, Mark
N [water]		Nile, phone
O [quail chick]		moon, float
[vulture]		pot, Oliver, Molly
P [stool]		pet, Pete
PH [horned viper]		pharaoh, Caleph
Q [basket & quail chick together]		queen, Quentin, Quinita
R [open mouth]		rain, ribbon, Rachel, Robin

Hieroglyph		Sound
S [folded cloth]		house, sand, Iris, Sandy
SH [lake]		ship, Sheryl, Asher
T [bread loaf]		tell, Teddy, Tina
TH [cow's belly]		through, Seth
[unknown]		the, Thelma, Theo
U [quail chick]		cut, full, Aretha, Cully, Cubby
[one reed leaf & quail chick]		mule, fuel, Eunice, Susan
V [horned viper]		video, Victoria
W [quail chick]		wind, cow, what, Wendy, Walter
X [basket & folded cloth together]		box, extra, Axel, Xavier, Roxanne, Alex
Y [one reed leaf]		you, yes, Yolanda
[two reed leaves]		Mary, Yvonne
Z [door bolt]		zebra, Zena, Ziggy

Make a Cartouche

A cartouche (car-TOOSH) is an oval or oblong-shaped sign containing a name written in hieroglyphics. Create a cartouche with your name from air-drying or oven-drying clay. A cartouche makes a nice gift for someone else, too. You can even add a secret message that only you and a friend can read.

Form a ball with the clay by rolling it in the palm of your hand until it is smooth and round, or egg–shaped—whichever you prefer.

Pat the clay to form a flat circle or oval (as if you were making a hamburger). On the back, scoop out a small indentation for a nail or picture hanger, so you can hang it on a wall when you're done. On the front, form the hieroglyphs, using a nail.

You don't have to use vowels—the ancient Egyptians often left them out. If your name is Jenn, for instance, you would find the sounds of "J" and "N." Place the letters artistically, going up or down, backward or forward. That's how the ancients did it.

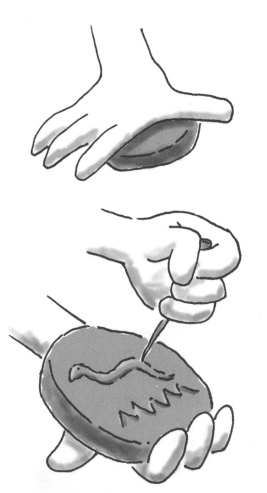

Kn U Rd Ths Msage?

Here is a message from us to you, written in hieroglyphs:

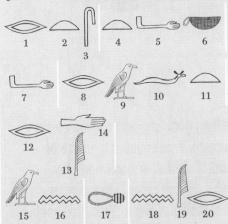

Can you decode it? Now try writing some secret messages of your own using the hieroglyphic alphabet on page 60.

The Rosetta Stone

Long after ancient Egypt ceased to exist as a country, people looked at the hieroglyphics and wondered what those little pictures could possibly mean.

It wasn't until one of Napoleon's soldiers found a special stone in the town of Rosetta in 1798 that the hieroglyphic code was broken.

A royal announcement was on the stone and it was written in both Greek and in hieroglyphics. Jean Champollion, a French scholar, finally broke the code. When Champollion was just 11 years old, his parents had taken him on a trip to the pyramids at Giza. Supposedly, he stood in front of the mysterious hieroglyphics and declared, "Someday, I'm going to find out what they mean!"

Twenty-five years later, he became world-famous for doing just that. Talk about the power of intention! Hats off to Champollion—and any other person who fulfills a childhood dream!

Think About It:

Setting goals makes your life easier because it gives you a measure of control. And your goals don't have to be difficult or as long-range as Champollion's either. Your goal might be to eat healthier foods, to learn a new skill, or to become friends with people in your class who are from a different culture. Set a reasonable goal today and then think about how you can make it happen.

TRACES OF THE PAST

The African-Asian language that the ancient Egyptians used is long gone, but traces of it remain in words we use today.

The "chem" in chemistry, for instance, comes from the ancient name for Egypt, "Khem." Egypt was called Khem which means black as in the "Black Land" (the fertile soil near the Nile). Since the people of ancient Egypt were the first to do chemical experiments in their attempts to cure illnesses and preserve the bodies of mummies, the word chemistry evolved from them.

The word luxury comes to us from ancient Egypt, too. The palaces and temples in the ancient city of Luxur were so beautiful that the word luxury has come to mean anything rich and grand.

My Dear Mummy

The people of ancient Egypt imagined life after this life as a happy continuation of sunny days, riverboat rides, tasty food, friendships, and fun. (See page 40.) The key to getting to this afterlife, or eternal life, they believed, was through the body. The ancients thought a person's soul, or ka as it was called, would live only as long as the body was preserved. Over time, the people of ancient Egypt came to believe that drying a body was a way to preserve the person's life and soul, as well as the body.

THE FIRST MUMMIES

The first Egyptian mummies were the bodies of people who had been buried in the desert. These bodies dried out and remained whole through a natural process—that is, nobody preserved them. A mummy is a dried human, the way a raisin is a dried grape.

The process of keeping a body from decaying is called mummification. To make a mummy, the dead person's body would be carefully emptied of everything—except the heart—and then refilled with sawdust and good–smelling spices. The body was set in a kind of salt to dry. Good luck charms, called amulets, were added as the body was wrapped in layers of linen. When all this was done, the mummy would be placed in a special coffin, called a sarcophagus (sar-KOF-a-gus), decorated with his or her image.

The body parts that were removed were kept in special urns, each under the protection of a special god. Oddly, the brain was the only body part that was thrown away!

Think About It:

In preparing the mummy the heart wasn't removed, but the brain was both removed and thrown away! What does this tell you about the ancients' sense of importance and ideas about what makes a good life?

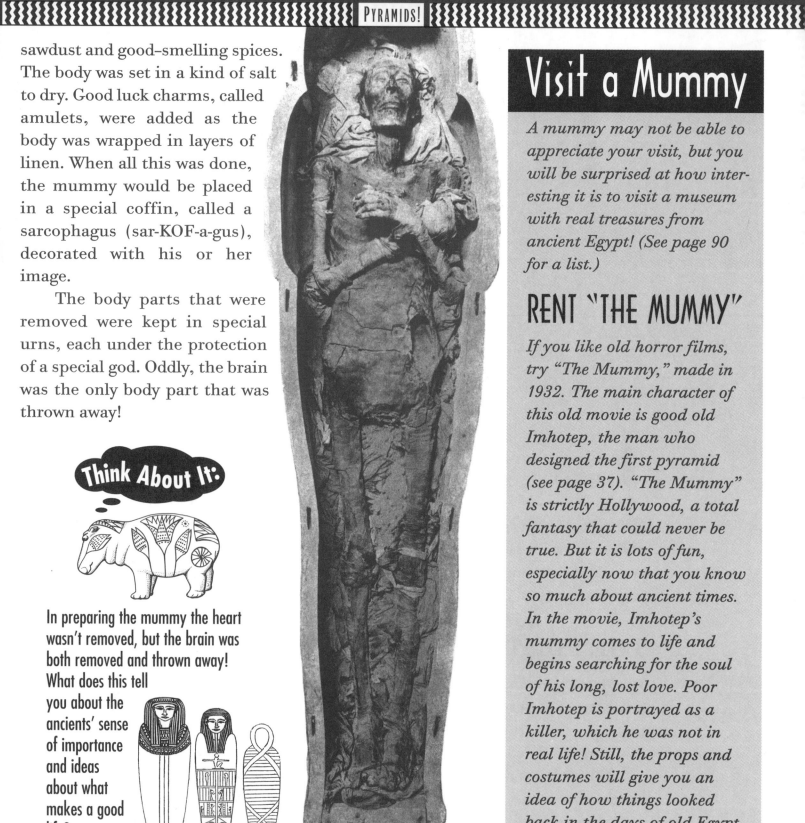

Visit a Mummy

A mummy may not be able to appreciate your visit, but you will be surprised at how interesting it is to visit a museum with real treasures from ancient Egypt! (See page 90 for a list.)

RENT "THE MUMMY"

If you like old horror films, try "The Mummy," made in 1932. The main character of this old movie is good old Imhotep, the man who designed the first pyramid (see page 37). "The Mummy" is strictly Hollywood, a total fantasy that could never be true. But it is lots of fun, especially now that you know so much about ancient times. In the movie, Imhotep's mummy comes to life and begins searching for the soul of his long, lost love. Poor Imhotep is portrayed as a killer, which he was not in real life! Still, the props and costumes will give you an idea of how things looked back in the days of old Egypt.

Make a Soul House Model

When archaeologists entered the tombs of ancient Egypt, they were surprised to see little models of objects from everyday life formed from clay. It seems the people of those days believed that there was magical power to making models, as if the gods would create what the model showed.

A soul house was a special kind of model, a little home for the ka — the part of the soul that they believed lived longer than the body. Soul houses were small and made of clay, but they had details like stairways and pillars, and even tiny baskets of bread. In the pyramids, there were models of boats, soldiers, cattle, and people playing, dancing, and partying.

Use air–drying or oven–baked clay to make a lasting model of a soul house for yourself. You can model a scene from ancient Egypt, or of your life today. Another way to create a soul house is with a shoe box. You can decorate the inside of the box as a copy of your room — either as it is, or as you would want it to be in the Land of Forever.

TEST AT THE GATE OF THE UNDERWORLD

To achieve life everlasting, the ancient Egyptians believed people had to be deserving: They had to have kind hearts.

They believed that after death, the god Osiris and his daughter Maat, who was the goddess of truth, would meet you to weigh your heart. The heart was put on one side of a scale, with Maat's Feather of Truth on the other scale. Forty-two gods

and goddesses would then interview the heart, asking it about any crimes it may have committed. Maat would know for sure if anyone was lying.

If the heart was light, with no hate, the person would gain eternal life. If the heart was heavy, with hate and mean deeds, the fierce goddess Ammut, part-crocodile, part-lion, and part-hippo, would devour it on the spot!

BOOKS OF INSTRUCTION

To help people learn to become wise and good, Books of Instruction were written by wise people in old Egypt. Here is a sample from a book written thousands of years ago:

If a poor person owes you something, take only a third of what he owes and let him keep the rest. If you do this you will sleep well at night and wake up feeling good. It is much better to be praised for your neighborly love than to have riches in the storeroom.

Think About It:

The goddess Maat, the sun-god's daughter, stands for a perfect world, in perfect order. Her symbol was an ostrich feather. Maat was both a goddess and an important idea. The people of old Egypt believed that if everyone would live according to Maat, being truthful and doing what they were supposed to do with a good attitude, then the whole world would run smoothly and people would be truly happy.

What do you think about the idea that Maat stands for? If there were such a thing as Maat, what would those ideals be in your life? In your home? In your school? Do you think that your friends or people in a different part of the world would describe the goodness and perfection of Maat as you do?

Think About It:

Think of a basic truth about being a good person; then write a statement for your own book of instructions. Ask your friends to trade some back and forth until you come up with a complete guidebook to being a good, helpful, and trustworthy person.

WHAT A RELIEF!

All the pictures of the heart test on pyramid walls show people passing the test with flying colors and going on to the Land of Forever.

The people of old Egypt believed deeply in the power of forgiveness. In their religion, it was not good to hold onto bad feelings like anger or guilt. If someone did something wrong but felt sorry about it, the ancients believed that the gods instantly forgave the person. The priests and the pharaohs also urged people to forgive each other quickly when things went wrong between them.

When ideas are right, they don't have to change. The ancient Egyptian idea of a good person—someone who is honest, forgiving, and kind—is as fine an idea today as it was thousands of years ago.

WEIGH YOUR HEART

Thinking about having a heart free of anger and hate is a useful and good thing to do. Do you have any bad feelings you are ready to set free? Forgiving people who have done wrong to us makes our hearts light and free.

Test your power of forgiveness by making a list of people who make you angry. When your list is finished, ask yourself if you have been angry long enough and can now forgive the person. (If you have a hard time even thinking about forgiving the person, try forgiving yourself for being so angry and upset. That sometimes works just as well.)

When you have gone over your list, look at each name, close your eyes, and murmur these magical words:

"(Name), we are even. I fully forgive you and free myself now."

Cross out the name on the list and go on to the next one. When your list is all crossed out, roll it into a ball and throw it away. Hey! We can practically see the big smile of relief on your face already!

Temper Tantrums Egyptian-Style

When a woman had a baby in ancient times, she would sit on a special little stool during the birth. That stool was then given to the newborn to keep all his or her life — for a very strange reason. Whenever the person became angry, he or she could hit or kick the stool!

This custom may have given the usually barefoot Egyptians an occasional sore toe, but it certainly allowed them to get their bad feelings out without hurting anyone!

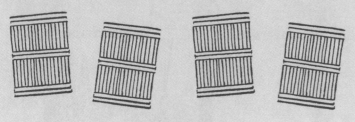

Think About It:

What are some good ways for you to release angry feelings and tension without hurting yourself or anyone else? Since we all get angry at times, it is good for each of us to have a plan to release that anger safely. Maybe you like to punch the pillows on your bed or scream in the shower or go outside and take five deep, deep breaths. Whatever works for you and doesn't hurt anyone, is a good plan.

The Curse of the Mummy

Note: Here is a story based on true facts. Two Englishmen, the wealthy Lord Carnarvon and archaeologist Howard Carter, really did visit the pyramids. They discovered King Tut's treasure in 1915. (See page 37.)

Howard Carter leaned on his shovel and shook his head in discouragement. "We've been searching for King Ramses' tomb for two years now, and we've found nothing but dirt and dust!"

"Perhaps we should go back to England," his friend, Lord Carnarvon suggested.

"Go back? No! I won't admit defeat!" Suddenly, Carter spied something oval-shaped in the hill of sand and dust. "What's this?" he asked, dusting it with the small brush he carried to remove the sands of time. "Look here! It's a royal seal!"

"And in those rocks next to it, I believe I see an outline, Carter," Carnarvon replied, his face brightening. "By Jove, it's a door!"

Carter set to work clearing debris away from the ancient stone door. Inside was a dusty, empty room. "Drat! It looks like grave robbers beat us to the punch."

"Carter! Come here!" cried Carnarvon, who was holding a candle. "Look through this little hole!"

Peering through the hole, Carter spied a golden chariot!

"Boss!" cried another worker excitedly. "Come see!" The worker had found another small opening leading to another room. Looking into that opening, Carter saw a golden throne!

"A royal throne! This is it!" Carter cried happily.

As the workers opened up the rooms of the tomb, the dazzling riches of a pharaoh appeared in all their splendor. There were urns made of solid gold, chariots, boats, and furniture fit for a king.

"According to the hieroglyphics on the wall, we're in one of King Tutankhamen's chambers," Carter whispered in awe, turning to his partner. "He was the youngest king of all. Just think, Carnarvon, all this treasure now belongs to us!"

Behind Carter, one of the workers frowned. "This ancient treasure rightfully belongs to the people of Egypt," he whispered bitterly to the man next to him.

Despite the amazing discovery, Lord Carnarvon appeared to be quite miserable. "Perhaps it's the dust, but I'm suddenly feeling ill," he said quietly.

The two returned to the capital of modern Egypt, the city of Cairo, only to find there had been a power outage just when the tomb had been discovered.

Carter took his friend to different doctors.

"I don't know what's the matter with him. Perhaps he was bitten by a poisonous mosquito," one doctor suggested half-heartedly.

"I honestly cannot tell what this strange illness is," another admitted.

The next day, Carnarvon died. The Egyptian newspapers said: "Lord Carnarvon — Victim of the Curse of the Mummy!"

"Death comes on swift wings to those who disturb the rest of the Pharaoh!" one article read. The reporters claimed that the quote was written on the pyramid walls.

"Rubbish! I'm not superstitious," Carter said confidently. "I will continue exploring until I find King Tut's tomb!"

Weeks later, Carter found King Tut's burial room.

"Boss, don't go in there," one of his workers warned. Many others quit on the spot. But that didn't stop Carter.

In the burial room were four coffins and several statues. One of the statues had this warning: "I, who drive back the robbers of the tomb with the flames of the desert, I am the Protector of Tutankhamen's tomb!"

On the day the tomb was opened, far away in London, at the exact same moment, Carter's dog howled loudly and died.

Of the twenty people standing with Carter when the Pharaoh's sarcophagus was opened, thirteen were dead within a year.

Were all these problems just a series of coincidences? Or was it…the Curse of the Mummy?

You decide.

Fact or Fiction?

To help you decide if the Curse of the Mummy is real, consider these ideas:

1. Most people are uncomfortable being in graveyards, funeral parlors, or tombs.

2. When Carter and Carnarvon claimed ownership of the royal Egyptian treasures, many Egyptians became angry. The government sent soldiers to temporarily lock Carter out.

3. During the days when Carter was locked out, the London and American newspapers had a problem. What could they write for all the readers who were dying to find out more about Tut's treasure? (Sorry, we couldn't resist that one.)

The papers began publishing anything at all—even information that wasn't accurate. The quote about death coming on swift wings, for instance, was made up by an American writer.

4. Lord Carnarvon had been sick for a long time. He had traveled to Egypt in the first place because his doctors had advised him to get away from the damp English weather.

5. When Carnarvon scratched a bite on his face, it became infected. This infection led to pneumonia.

6. Power outages were very common in Cairo in those days.

7. The people who worked with Carter were older, more experienced workers who lived very hard lives. Their death rates were no different from other older workers.

8. Carnarvon's dog was 13 years old when he died.

9. The real words on the walls of the tomb talked about how welcome friendly visitors would be! In the days of ancient Egypt, robbing a tomb was a sin, but visiting was an act of kindness. (Of course, Carnarvon and Carter were robbing the tomb, in a way.)

10. In the Egyptian religion, people were not allowed to hurt others even if someone committed a crime. Punishment was supposed to come from the gods—not from human beings, dead or alive!

So, do you think the Curse of the Mummy is true?

Think About It:

Do you believe everything you read in the newspapers or see on TV?

Old Superstitions

Curses and superstitions are beliefs that have no reason or logic to them. You have probably heard of many superstitions, like the one about Friday the 13th being unlucky. What are some of the superstitions you have heard? Do you think they are true or false? Here is a list we made to get you started:

True or false: Step on a crack, break your mother's back.

(If this were true, all mothers would have broken backs!)

True or false: Black cats bring bad luck.

(Our black cat, Hubert, brought us nothing but joy and cuddly happiness.)

True or false: Never walk under a ladder.

(Well, this one probably has some truth to it. It's not a good idea to walk under a ladder if someone is on it, or you might wind up with a can of paint on your head!)

Think About It:

On the other hand... some superstitions can be pleasant. They don't harm anyone and may even do some good. If someone has a lucky hat, for instance, they may feel good wearing it. It is just a way to boost self-confidence, but it is harmless and fun. Have you ever had a lucky charm?

CHARMS AND AMULETS

Imagine having a trinket that would help you attract all the good things you want — good luck, good times, good thoughts, and good friends. The ancients believed that carrying or wearing amulets, or charms, would protect them from trouble and guide them to good experiences.

Many people all over the world still wear charms and amulets today. They feel stronger or more secure with a special object in their pocket or around their neck.

But will a charm or amulet really bring special power and good luck? Find out by using one! What if they work only because a person really believes in them? That's still an amazing power, isn't it?

Make Your Own Amulet

When you choose a charm or amulet, think about a trinket that would remind you of what you want. A bird might stand for the feeling of freedom, or the sun might stand for warm, *friendly people. A pyramid or moon could stand for secret wisdom, and a star might remind you that you are a special, one-of-a-kind person.*

You can hide your charm *under a shirt or show it off for everyone to see.*

In ancient Egypt, the symbol for life was the ankh (see page 53). You can form a good-luck ankh from air-drying clay or oven-drying plastic. Tie it onto a piece of yarn and wear it to attract good luck.

Another popular charm was the Eye of Horus, designed to keep away evil, and attract joy.

Whatever you choose, for good luck or decoration, we are certain that if you think good thoughts about yourself and others and if your heart is light and free of worry, all will go well with you.

EYE OF
HORUS

MEET PHARAOH: AT THE TOP OF THE PYRAMID

On the news, the announcer sometimes says, "The White House announced today that...." News in England sometimes begins, "According to 10 Downing Street...." Of course, neither the White House nor 10 Downing Street can talk—they are buildings! The words "White House" stand for the President of the United States, just as 10 Downing Street stands for the Prime Minister of England. Our custom of calling the head of the country by the place he or she lives comes from ancient Egypt, where the words per aa or pharaoh meant Great House. The personal name of the pharaoh, who was the most royal Egyptian, was thought to be too holy and important for ordinary people to utter.

WHO WAS PHARAOH?

He—or she—was thought to be a living god, the earthly representative of the all-powerful sun god, Amun-Re. Every morning, just as the dawn was about to break, pharaoh went to the temple and commanded, "Rise in peace, great one!"

In temples, all over Egypt, other priests did the same in the pharaoh's name. Some people believed that if pharaoh didn't call on the sun to shine, there would be no sun at all that day!

The laws of ancient Egypt were based on what pharaoh

thought was right or wrong. He or she was the head judge and lawmaker. Usually, a pharaoh was the first son of a reigning pharaoh. If a pharaoh had no sons, the man who married his daughter could become pharaoh if he were well respected. Sometimes, strong-willed queens worked their way into the position.

In the rich society of ancient Egypt, the pharaoh was by far the wealthiest citizen and lived in unbelievable luxury. He or she was supported by everyone in the Two Lands of Egypt. The poorest farmers had to give pharaoh a portion of their crops, workers donated their labor, and artists created art for pharaoh.

And all in all, it seems that the people of ancient Egypt didn't mind giving to their royalty. By giving generously they believed that the goddess Maat would bless their lives with peace and contentment. (See page 65.)

Think About It:

Imagine the most kind-hearted, honest person. Then give that person the power to control all things—religion, wealth, jobs, the law, punishment. What kinds of problems, or conflicts, might arise when one person has so much power?

The Pharaoh Position: Royal Posture At Work

The ancient Egyptians were the first people to put arms on chairs, making the first armchairs for thrones for their kings and queens. Even today, sitting up straight in a chair and resting your arms is thought by some to promote clear thinking.

Is this true? Try it to find out!

A Pyramid Power Structure

The people of ancient Egypt were organized like an imaginary pyramid with the pharaoh in power and the peasants having little of anything. Everyone had a place in the chain of command that started at the top. Pharaoh was at the tip, followed by his assistants, priests, and officials of the provinces, such as tax collectors and scribes. Next came soldiers, artists, craftsmen, and then farmers and peasants.

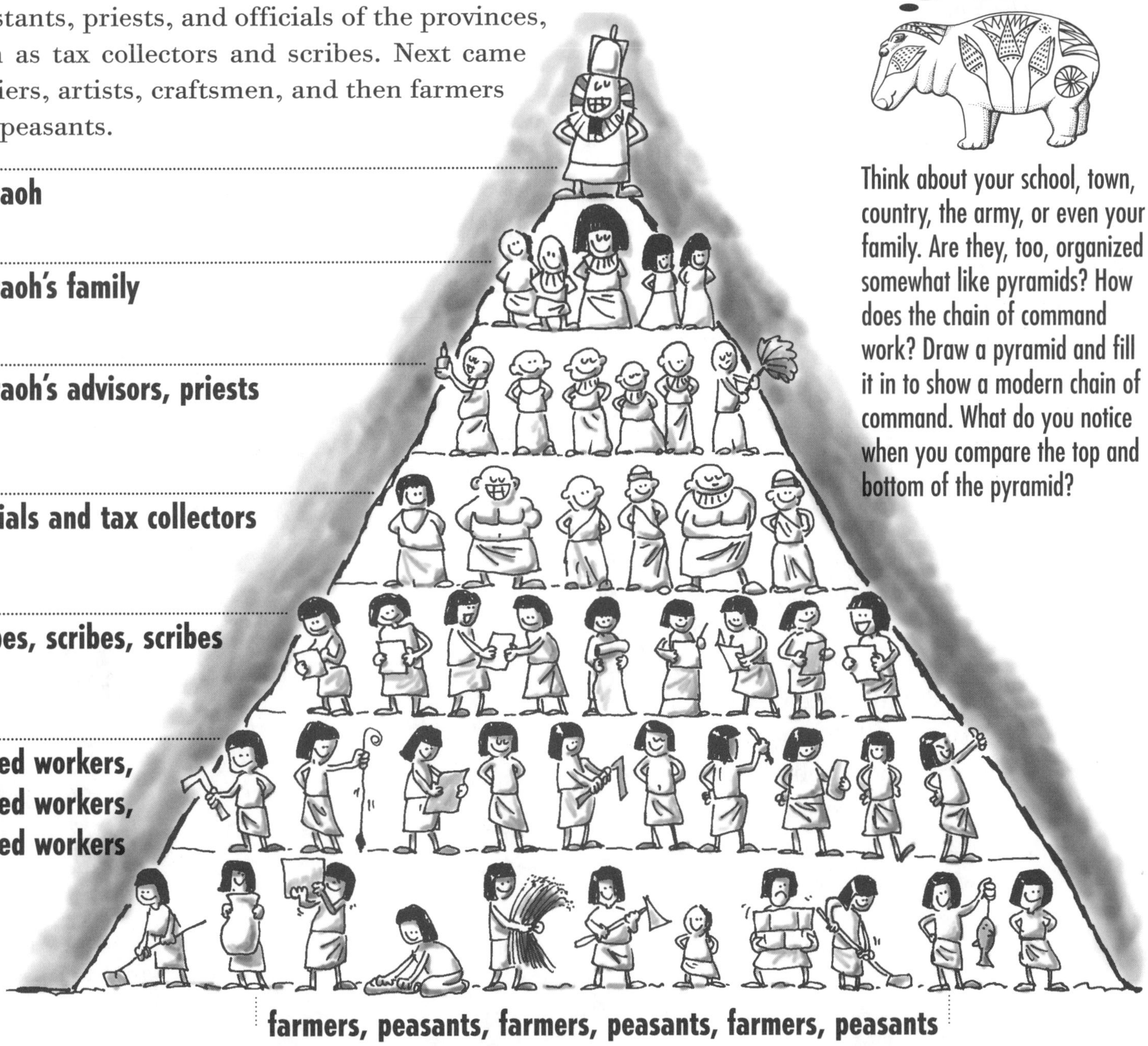

pharaoh

pharaoh's family

pharaoh's advisors, priests

officials and tax collectors

scribes, scribes, scribes

skilled workers, skilled workers, skilled workers

farmers, peasants, farmers, peasants, farmers, peasants

Think About It:

Think about your school, town, country, the army, or even your family. Are they, too, organized somewhat like pyramids? How does the chain of command work? Draw a pyramid and fill it in to show a modern chain of command. What do you notice when you compare the top and bottom of the pyramid?

THE DARK SIDE OF EGYPT

Although it seems that old Egypt was basically a healthy and stable society, there were sometimes problems, too. Think about the pyramid structure and imagine what it would be like if the person on top was selfish and unkind. What if the person on top lived in incredible luxury, but the people on the bottom had too little?

CROWN YOURSELF PHARAOH!

Imagine a king or queen so powerful that he or she wore two crowns! That was what King Narmer did when he united both parts of Egypt back in 3000 B.C. (see page 28).

The White Crown stood for Upper Egypt, in the South, and the Red Crown stood for Lower Egypt, in the north. Wearing both crowns showed Narmer's royal respect for both parts of the land.

There were other crowns in ancient Egypt, too – about 20 of them! Unlike the golden crowns of European kings, Egyptian crowns were each one-of-a-kind with only one detail shared by all of them: All the Egyptian crowns had a cobra's head sticking out in front, to show the wisdom and power of royalty.

RED CROWN

WHITE CROWN

BOTH CROWNS

Think About It:

Can you think of other ways of organizing people so that everyone has equal power? What shape would that take?

TOO MUCH POWER?

The pharaohs were worshipped as gods who would never die. Can you imagine being raised to believe that you were that powerful? Do you think you would believe it was really true? Do you think the pharaohs truly believed that they were gods? What would you do with all of that power today?

Make the White Crown of Upper Egypt

The white crown was shaped something like a bowling pin, and the person who wore it had total power.

YOU WILL NEED:

▷ **roll of waxed paper**
▷ **tape or glue**
▷ **scissors**
▷ **feathers and gold discs (optional)**

Wrap a piece of waxed paper 3 times around your head. Tape it so it stands tall. To make the knob on top (remember the bowling ball?), hold your fist in the center of the column, and gently shape the top of the waxed paper into a small knob.

Sometimes, feathers and round golden discs were added to the white crown to stand for Horus, the Falcon, (see page 50) and the sun. Add sun discs made from gold or yellow paper, and glue to the crown.

Make the Red Crown of Lower Egypt

The red crown is like a puffy, round, red living room chair. But it's a chair that sits on a very powerful head!

YOU WILL NEED:

▷ **red poster board (3 pieces of red construction paper taped together)**

▷ **scissors**

▷ **tape or glue**

Draw the outline of the red crown, as pictured on this page. Cut the shape from the poster board to fit your head. Tape on the inside.

Add a Silver Cobra

To make the distinctive cobra that is part of all Egyptian crowns, cut a long length of foil and fold the entire length of it in half the long way. Next, fold the foil again, this time in thirds—but leave several inches (centimeters) with just the first fold at the end. This is going to be the head of your cobra.

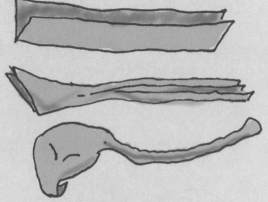

Fold in the tip of the wider end of the foil, leaving a few inches wide for the cobra's head. Shape the cobra's mouth by rolling the end of the foil. When you have a silver cobra, form the body into a circle and place it around the crown. Or, you can also put the body of the snake under your crown, with just the head sticking out.

THE ROYAL BEARD AND TAIL

When a pharaoh led a ceremony, part of the attire was a make-believe beard and tail! Even female pharaohs, like beautiful Queen Hatshepsut, wore both a beard and tail! We don't know exactly why pharaohs wore the false beards, which were usually blue—that piece of history is still a mystery. But the tail, like the cobra's head, seems to be there to remind others of pharaoh's magical, animal powers.

Pharaoh also carried a shepherd's staff and flail (whip). The staff reminded people that pharaoh was a protective shepherd. The flail reminded them that they'd better do what he liked!

Finding the right shoes was easy. Even the most royal royals usually went barefoot!

THE NEMES: BASEBALL CAP OF ANCIENT ROYALTY

One of the traditions of Egyptian royalty was that they could never let their natural hair be seen. For this reason they needed their heads covered at all times in public. Egyptian royalty only wore their crowns for important ceremonies, so for everyday wear, they wore a cloth headdress called the nemes. Even the sphinx wears a nemes!

Make a Nemes

Gold-on-gold striped upholstery fabric makes a very classy nemes, but wide red-and-white striped cotton looks good, too. In a pinch, you can even make your nemes from a pillow case (try painting it with fabric paint first)!

 YOU WILL NEED:

> ¹/4 yd (**22.5 cm**) striped fabric, the stiffer the better
> piece of gold trim
> safety pins or iron-on glue (like **Stitch Witchery®**)
> foil

Center the fabric on your forehead, covering your hair. Pull the material tightly across your forehead and fold the sides down in back of your ears. Pin the cloth at the folds.

Form a 6" (15 cm) square piece of foil into a cobra by folding it and shaping with your hands (see page 79). Set the cobra in the middle of your forehead and glue the gold trim over it, across the entire forehead.

Cut the hanging flaps of the nemes in a U shape.

Throw an Ancient Egyptian Costume Party

The people of ancient Egypt were truly party people! They loved a good time and seemed to have as many festivals and celebrations as possible. At the party, they'd enjoy food, acrobatics, music, and dancing. The ancient Egyptians practically invented partying!

So put on your red and white crowns, nemes, jewelry, and Egyptian clothes — and party like the pharaohs!

Make a Manly Kilt

Ancient Egyptian men and boys wore white linen kilts. You can make a simple kilt with a piece of white fabric, like an old sheet. You will need a package of safety pins, too.

Cut a piece of cloth that can go around your waist two and a half times and is long enough to reach from your waist to your knees. Fold pleats into the cloth, one by one, using safety pins. (The pleats should be about as wide as your pinky.) When the cloth is completely pleated, attach it around your waist. Cut a narrower strip of cloth to use as a sash.

Men also wore animal skins. How about getting some leopard-spotted or tiger-striped material at the fabric store and winding it around your waist as a loin cloth?

And don't forget, you may want to party in the pharaoh's garb!

FOLD AND PIN

FOLD AND PIN

TUCK

Create A Queen's Gown

Royalty and rich people of ancient Egypt wore white clothing, made of the finest linen. The women looked beautiful and the men looked handsome as they held their bodies straight and proud (see page 84).

To make a dress that a female pharaoh or fine Egyptian lady would wear, use an old white sheet or piece of white fabric. You will need a piece that winds around you two and a half times, reaching from your armpits to below your knees.

Attach the cloth by folding the top over and pinning underneath with a large safety pin. Use a strip of fabric as a sash.

Boogie barefoot in your Egyptian dress!

JEWELRY, JEWELRY, JEWELRY

While people in Europe were living in the drab Stone Age, the people of Egypt were creating a sleek style of their own that still looks good even today. Ancient Egyptians loved dressing up and wearing all kinds of beautiful jewelry, headbands, and headdresses. For parties, they'd wear wigs or carefully combed and braided hair. (In ancient times, uncombed hair was strictly for barbarians!)

Both women and men wore earrings, and bracelets on their upper and lower arms. They wore rings, necklaces, and pectorals, too. (Pectorals are wide necklaces, or jewelry that is worn on the chest.)

It is easy and fun to make fake jewelry with yarn, macaroni, watercolors, foil, glitter, and stickers.

Think About It:

Now that you know so much about ancient Egypt and the people of that time long ago, why do you think that they enjoyed social events, playing games, and partying so much? When do you most enjoy going to a party?

The Posture of the People of Old Egypt

Think About It:

Whether they worked in the fields or in palaces, ancient Egyptians moved with dignity and grace. Judging from the ancient art they left behind, their bodies were straight and strong, with heads held high, shoulders wide, and feet firmly on the ground.

Do you think this posture reflects their sense of being happy with life? Do you think the way a person holds his or her body makes a difference in how that person feels?

Slump your shoulders over and hang your head down. Does this feel like a happy or sad way to hold your body? Now gently lift up your head and neck, and make your shoulders relaxed and wide. How does this posture feel?

Pretend to walk like a beaten-down person, and then change and walk like a royal king or queen. Was there a change in how you held your body? We bet there was!

Use Your Head to Carry Something

Maybe one of the reasons that the ancient Egyptians had such beautiful posture is that they used their heads to carry things. Our heads and necks can be very strong if we hold them the right way.

To test this method of carrying, try walking with a book or basket of towels on top of your head. You will only be able to do it if you carry your head and body upright and move smoothly.

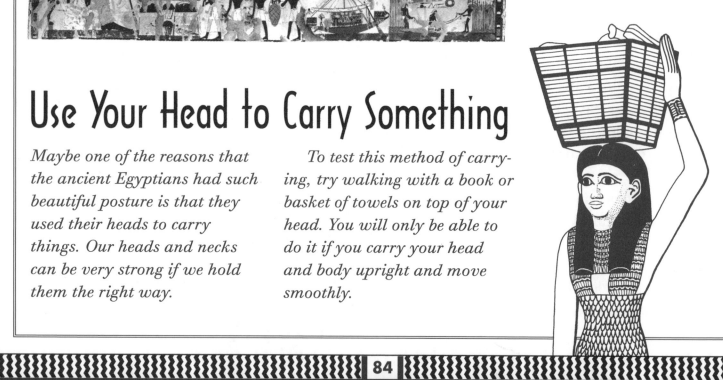

Party Food

Chances are you won't be able to serve hippopotamus at your party like an ancient Egyptian might have. Eating hippopotamus is one tradition that did not survive through history!

A PLATTER FULL OF SWEET FRUITS

Grapes, figs, dates, apples, melons, pomegranates, and the occasional coconut — these are the fruits ancient Egyptians enjoyed, so they are the perfect fruits to serve at your party.

You probably don't have a pet monkey or baboon who can pick the fruit off the trees for you, the way the ancient Egyptians had, but if it's ripe, the fruit will still taste good!

Eating etiquette:

Cut the fruit into slices that can be eaten with fingers. There were no forks or spoons in ancient Egypt. People ate with the tips of their fingers, and everyone was given a little bowl of water to dip their hands into after the meal.

Bake Honey-Barley Flatbread

Barley is a strength-giving grain. It's one of the foods that made life possible for the earliest humans! The pyramid builders ate unsweetened flatbread made with barley every day.

For your party, how about baking a sweet barley flatbread? (You can buy barley flour in a health food store.)

Here is a recipe that uses ingredients that are as old as time.

1 cup (250 ml) barley flour
1/4 cup (50 ml) water
1/3 cup (75 ml) honey
1 tablespoon (15 ml) oil

Mix together and pour into a small oiled pan. Bake for 20-30 minutes in a hot oven (375° F or 190° C). The cake will be flat and dark because barley doesn't rise and it darkens when it bakes.

Add a handful of raisins, cut-up figs, or shredded coconut to the batter for an extra treat. Egyptians ate those things, too!

Dance Like an Egyptian

The instruments of ancient Egypt were instruments meant for blowing and plucking. We can see them pictured on the pyramid walls, but we can only hear them in our imaginations. Your local music store probably has some tapes of modern-day Egyptian music to boogie to. We can only imagine how the Egyptians danced by looking at old

pictures. Since those pictures usually show things from the side, try making up an Egyptian dance by putting one arm in front of you and the other arm behind you.

For fun, if you can find the recording called "Walk Like An Egyptian" by The Bangles that was popular a few years back, play it at your party and dance Egyptian-style!

Play Senat— An Ancient Board Game

Long, long ago, Egyptians relaxed by playing Senat, which means "passing." This board game is the great–great–great–great grandfather of checkers. We cannot be exactly sure of how the game was played, but we know the object of Senat was the same as checkers — to capture the other player's pieces.

In Senat, the pieces are called kelb, and the squares are called ooyen, or eyes. The Egyptians sat on the floor, and played on a low table.

 **YOU WILL NEED:**

▹ **square piece of stiff cardboard**
▹ **ruler**
▹ **black marker or felt-tip pen**
▹ **two sets of 12 checkers (better yet, smooth pebbles) to be the kelb**

To make the board: Draw 25 squares on the cardboard by drawing 4 lines in both directions. Mark an X in the center square. The 25 spaces are the ooyen.

To set the board: The youngest player goes first, placing two kelb, or pieces, anywhere on the board, except the middle ooyen, which is left empty until the game begins. Then the other player sets two kelb down, and both players take turns until all the pieces are on the board. HINT: Try to put your kelb on the outer edges.

RULES OF THE GAME:

1. Kelb can be moved one space forward, backward, or sideways. They cannot jump or move diagonally.

2. Kelb are captured (and removed) when the other player traps you between two of her pieces. NOTE: If you voluntarily move between two of your opponent's pieces, your kelb cannot be taken!

3. If you capture a kelb, take another turn, and keep on taking turns as long as you capture kelb.

4. If you cannot move, you lose your turn. However, the other player has to open up a space for your next move.

5. To begin, the youngest player moves a kelb onto the middle (X) space.

6. The game is over when a player cannot move, or has no kelb left. The winner is the player with the most captured kelb.

Then and Now:
An Ancient Egyptian Song

On the walls of a pyramid is a picture of a blind harpist, singing at a party. The song is about life, and it tells how some ancients must have felt deep inside.

Song of the Blind Harpist

Spend a pleasant day!
Be good to yourself in every way.
Wear sweet oil and fine linen
And feel the miracle in All of Life.
Enjoy yourself every day,
Do what you have to do,
Without complaining.
Because no one comes back
From the land of the dead
To calm our hearts.
So let your heart be strong,
Make yourself happy,
Celebrate your life today.

THE MESSAGE FROM ANCIENT TIMES

Visiting a long ago and faraway place like ancient Egypt is like exploring a long forgotten part of ourselves. That's because the ancient ways remind us of what's really important: work, play, love, friendship, the rhythm of nature, and the flowing river of time.

By taking part in the activities and experiences in this book, you have connected our information to your imagination. Now, when you travel, in time or space, you'll bring a piece of ancient Egypt with you!

Think About It:

As you read the words of the song, ask yourself: What was important to the blind harpist? Was he convinced that Egyptians would live again after they died? What line or lines have the most meaning to you today? Is the message of the ancient blind harpist still valuable to our view of life and death today?

ANSWERS

From page 23: *The number of generations is 200. Now that is a long, long, long, long, long… time ago!*

From page 30: *Here is the answer to the riddle of the Sphinx:*

A human walks on four legs in the morning—that is, as a baby he crawls; on two legs in the afternoon—as a child and an adult; and on three legs in the evening—using a cane when he is old!

From page 40: *They filled the empty hall with sand to stand on as they painted, and gradually emptied the sand from the room as they moved down the pillar.*

From page 41: *It would have taken 100,000 men 5 years to build the Great Pyramid. Did you notice one fact that was in the question just to confuse you?*

From page 58: *Symbols (left to right): water, basket, open mouth.*

Message: "Here's good advice: Be nice to your mummy."

From page 61: *Kn U Rd Ths Msage?: "Let's take a raft ride on the Nile."*

Museum Listings

The following museums have beautiful objects from ancient Egypt. Which is closest to where you live?

In the United States:

Albright–Knox Art Gallery *(Buffalo, New York)*
The Brooklyn Museum *(Brooklyn, New York)*
The Cleveland Museum of Art *(Cleveland, Ohio)*
The Detroit Institute *(Detroit, Michigan)*
JB Speed Art Museum *(Louisville, Kentucky)*
The Metropolitan Museum of Art *(New York, New York)*
Michael C. Carlos Museum *(Atlanta, Georgia)*
Museum of Fine Arts *(Boston, Massachusetts)*
Museum of Science and Natural History *(Little Rock, Arkansas)*
Rosicrucian Egyptian and Oriental Museum *(San Jose, California)*
The Toledo Museum of Art *(Toledo, Ohio)*
The University of Pennsylvania Museum *(Philadelphia, Pennsylvania)*
University of Illinois Classical and European Culture Museum *(Urbana, Illinois)*
The Virginia Museum of Fine Arts *(Richmond, Virginia)*
Western Reserve Historical Society *(Cleveland, Ohio)*
William Rockhill Nelson Art Gallery, Atkins Museum *(Kansas City, Missouri)*

In Europe and Africa:

Ashmolean Museum *(Oxford, England)*
Agyptisches Museum *(Berlin, Germany)*
The British Museum *(London, England)*
The Cairo Museum *(Cairo, Egypt)*
Fitzwilliam Museum *(Cambridge, England)*

Musée du Louvre *(Paris, France)*

Musées Royaux d'Art et d'Histoire *(Brussels, Belgium)*

The Royal Scottish Museum *(Edinburgh, Scotland)*

Staatliche Sammlung Agyptischer Kunst *(Munich, Germany)*

University College *(London, England)*

Resources

Ancient Egypt, A Cultural Atlas for Young People by Geraldine Harris, Facts on File, Equinox Limit, Oxford, 1990.

The Egyptians by Anne Millard, Macdonald Educational Limited, 1975.

Egypt to the End of the Old Kingdom by Cyril Aldred, McGraw-Hill Book Co., 1965.

Exploring the Past: Ancient Egypt by George Hart, Harcourt Brace Jovanovich, 1988.

Finding Out About Ancient Egypt by H. Mellersh, Lothrop, Lee and Shepard, 1962.

Life of the Ancient Egyptians by Eugene Strouhal, University of Oklahoma Press, 1992.

Life Under the Pharaohs by Leonard Cottrell, Holt, Rhinehart and Winston, 1960.

Pyramid by David Macaulay, Houghton Mifflin Company, Boston, 1975.

Secrets of Tut's Tomb and the Pyramids by Stephanie Ann Reiff, Raintree Children's Books, 1977.

Tutankhamen's Gift by Robert Sabuda, MacMillan Publishing, 1994.

About the Archival Art

Page 14: *Man kneeling in the shade of a doum palm.*

Page 15: *Kachina doll, which represents supernatural spirits in many Pueblo Indian religions.*

Page 17: *Egyptian paddle doll.*

Page 22: *Wall painting of a man making a food offering to the gods.*

Page 27: *Goddess Hathor represented as a cow with a horned headress.*

Page 28: *Mural of two women eating fruit, one smelling lotus, at a banquet.*

Page 50: *Isis in a protective gesture with arms outstretched.*

Page 71: *Gold and carnelian bead necklace with mandrake fruit pendants.*

Page 74: *Mural of King Tutankhamen (seated) receiving Huy, governor of Ethiopia.*

Page 85: *Date palm with monkeys or baboons.*

Page 86: *Mural of female musicians playing (left to right) double flute, lute, and harp.*

Page 90: *Nekhbet, the vulture goddess, holding symbols of eternity.*

 INDEX

More Good Books from Williamson Publishing

Kaleidoscope Kids!

KALEIDOSCOPE KIDS® books for ages 7 to 14, are 96 pages, fully illustrated, 10 x 10, $12.95 US/$19.95 CAN.

THE LEWIS & CLARK EXPEDITION
Join the Corps of Discovery to Explore Uncharted Territory
by Carol A. Johmann

ANCIENT ROME!
Exploring the Culture, People & Ideas of This Powerful Empire
by Avery Hart and Sandra Gallagher

Benjamin Franklin Silver Award
GOING WEST!
Journey on a Wagon Train to Settle a Frontier Town
by Carol A. Johmann and Elizabeth J. Rieth

Children's Book Council Notable Book
WHO *REALLY* DISCOVERED AMERICA?
Unraveling the Mystery & Solving the Puzzle
by Avery Hart

Children's Book Council Notable Book
American Bookseller Pick of the Lists
KNIGHTS & CASTLES
50 Hands-On Activities to Experience the Middle Ages
by Avery Hart and Paul Mantell

ForeWord Magazine Book of the Year Finalist
SKYSCRAPERS!
Super Structures to Design & Build
by Carol A. Johmann

THE BEAST IN YOU!
Activities & Questions to Explore Evolution
by Marc McCutcheon

American Bookseller Pick of the Lists
Parent's Guide Children's Media Award
ANCIENT GREECE!
40 Hands-On Activities to Experience This Wondrous Age
by Avery Hart and Paul Mantell

American Bookseller Pick of the Lists
!MEXICO!
40 Activities to Experience Mexico Past and Present
by Susan Milord

Teachers' Choice Award
GEOLOGY ROCKS!
50 Hands-On Activities to Explore the Earth
by Cindy Blobaum

Parents' Choice Recommended
BRIDGES!
Amazing Structures to Design, Build & Test
by Carol A. Johmann and Elizabeth J. Rieth

More Award-Winning Books from Williamson Publishing

 Kids Can!

KIDS CAN!® books for ages 5 to 12 are each 160–176 pages, fully illustrated, trade paper, 11 x 8 1/2, $12.95 US/$19.95 CAN.

Parents Magazine Parents' Pick
Real Life Award
KIDS LEARN AMERICA!
Bringing Geography to Life with People, Places & History
by Patricia Gordon and Reed C. Snow

Parents' Choice Honor Award
THE KIDS' NATURAL HISTORY BOOK
Making Dinos, Fossils, Mammoths & More
by Judy Press

Parents' Choice Gold Award
American Bookseller Pick of the Lists
THE KIDS' MULTICULTURAL ART BOOK
Art & Craft Experiences from Around the World
by Alexandra M. Terzian

Parents' Choice Approved
Benjamin Franklin Best Multicultural Book Award
THE KIDS' MULTICULTURAL COOKBOOK
Food & Fun Around the World
by Deanna F. Cook

Awesome
OCEAN SCIENCE!
Investigating the Secrets of the Underwater World
by Cindy A. Littlefield

GREAT GAMES!
Ball, Board, Quiz & Word, Indoors & Out, for Many or Few!
by Sam Taggar

JAZZY JEWELRY
Power Beads, Crystals, Chokers, & Illusion and Tattoo Styles
by Diane Baker

Parents' Choice Recommended
Children's Digest Health Education Award
The Kids' Guide to FIRST AID
All about Bruises, Burns, Stings, Sprains & Other Ouches
by Karen Buhler Gale, R.N.

American Bookseller Pick of the Lists
Parents' Choice Approved
SUMMER FUN!
60 Activities for a Kid-Perfect Summer
by Susan Williamson

American Bookseller Pick of the Lists
Oppenheim Toy Portfolio Best Book Award
THE KIDS' SCIENCE BOOK
Creative Experiences for Hands-On Fun
by Robert Hirschfeld and Nancy White

Parents' Choice Recommended
THE KIDS' BOOK OF WEATHER FORECASTING
Build a Weather Station, "Read" the Sky & Make Predictions!
with meteorologist Mark Breen and Kathleen Friestad

Parents' Choice Recommended
The Kids' Guide to
MAKING SCRAPBOOKS & PHOTO ALBUMS!
How to Collect, Design, Assemble, Decorate
by Laura Check

Selection of Book-of-the-Month; Scholastic Book Clubs
KIDS COOK!
Fabulous Food for the Whole Family
by Sarah Williamson and Zachary Williamson

Parents' Choice Recommended
KIDS' ART WORKS!
Creating with Color, Design, Texture & More
by Sandi Henry